THE HEART OF NOTRE DAME: SPIRITUAL REFLECTIONS FOR STUDENTS, PARENTS, AND ALUMNI AND FRIENDS

THE HEART OF NOTRE DAME:

SPIRITUAL REFLECTIONS FOR STUDENTS, PARENTS, ALUMNI, AND FRIENDS

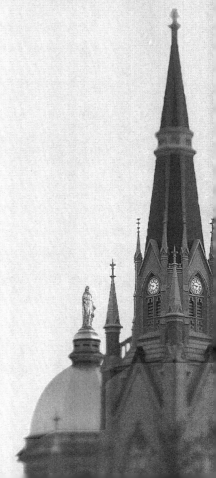

THE HEART OF NOTRE DAME:
Spiritual Reflections for
Students, Parents, Alumni, and Friends

Copyright © 2010 by Nicholas Ayo

10 9 8 7 6 5 4 3 2 1

ISBN 978-0-9827846-5-5

Published by
CORBY BOOKS
a Division of Corby Publishing, LP
P.O. Box 93
Notre Dame, IN 46556
11961 Tyler Road
Lakeville, IN 46536
574) 784-3482
corbypublishing.com

MANUFACTURED IN THE UNITED STATES OF AMERICA

TABLE OF CONTENTS

PREFACE

FOREWORD:
A CAUTIONARY TALE

THE CAMPUS

CHAPTER ONE – SOUNDINGS

1. What We Are Doing 3
2. Wisdom Comes With Age,
   and Maybe Love as Well.....................................7
3. Hobbits and Saints Marching In 10
4. Homeless.. 13
5. Lost Dreams 15
6. Retired 18
7. Old Age.. 21
8. What God Is Doing.. 24
9. Love Is Strong As Death 26
10. Real Presence 29

THE WOMEN

CHAPTER TWO – MYSTERIES

11. The Problem Of Evil.. 41
12. Brave New World.. 44

13. Brothers and Sisters, is There a God? 48

14. Sign of the Cross................................. 51

15. Fundamentalism.................................. 54

16. Silence without Noise.......................... 58

17. No Away No Way 61

18. How God Knows the Future.................... 64

19. Beyond Miracle 68

20. Trinity Mystery.................................. 72

21. The Christmas Crib............................. 76

22. No Triage in God 79

CHAPTER THREE
WONDERS

23. The Enchantment of the World 83

24. Dewfall Nostalgia.............................. 85

25. The Sacred Quadrant 87

26. How Does God Do It All? 90

27. Does God Suffer? 92

28. Given Time and Space.......................... 95

THE CROSS

CHAPTER FOUR
PRAYERS

29. Confession...................................... 109

30. The Woman Taken in Adultery.................. 112

31. Mercy and Forgiveness 115

32. Conversion and The Father of Mercies 118

33. How to Pray.................................... 120

34. Why Pray? 123

35. Can We Pray Always?........................... 126

36. Can Prayer Change Anything? 129

37. Morning Prayer 132

38. Evening Prayer 135

39. Eucharistic Prayer 138

40. Hail Mary 141

CHAPTER FIVE
SCRIPTURES

41. Saint Joseph 147

42. John the Baptist 150

43. The Grand Reunion 153

44. Mary Magdalene and the Many Marys 155

44. The Little Ones 158

45. Jepthah's Daughter 161

46. The Judas Story 163

47. The Widow Of Nain 167

48. The Lady on the Dome 170

49. Wheat and Weeds 173

50. Transfiguration 176

51. Loaves and Fishes 179

52. The Good Samaritan 182

53. The Mercy: A Reprise 185

CHAPTER SIX
ENGAGEMENTS

54. Marriage 193

55. Divorce 196

56. Passing on the Faith 199

57. The Priest as Memory of the Church 202

58. Jesus and Courtship 204

59. Did Jesus Marry? 207

60. Gay: Fine by Me: Wait a Minute 210

CHAPTER SEVEN
PONDERINGS

61. Lost Dreams Revisited 215

62. Old Age Revisited 218

63. The Meaning of Life
    Discovered in Old Age 221

64. Re-member 224

65. Caretakers 226

66. Regrets 228

67. What the Past has Said 232

68. So Few, So Much, So Many 235

69. Hidden Violence 238

70. Dorms for the Dead 240

71. My Own Death 243

72. Yes Or No 246

73. The Last Day 249

74. What the Future Might Say 252

THE BRICKS

ACKNOWLEDGMENTS

EVERY AUTHOR STANDS on the shoulders of those who educated him or her, and many others whose support and encouragement cannot be measured and without which this book would be much different or not at all. My family and friends, the Congregation of Holy Cross, and the University of Notre Dame come readily to mind. My editor and publisher, James Langford, has cultivated my writing career for twenty years. In particular I wish to thank my sister, Alida Macor, who read two times over the manuscript with a sharp and critical eye. The book is better for all such devotion, and the whatever shortcomings remain mine.

PREFACE

SEVERAL READERS of a previous book of mine that describes special places on the campus of Notre Dame told me they made a "retreat" with my book in hand. I was surprised, because *Signs of Grace* was written to promote a nostalgic walk around some of the intriguing scenes at Notre Dame – and nothing more. That the meditations in that book gave pause and led to prayerful reflection was not anticipated by the author, but it should have been. Visitors to Notre Dame, whether alums or residents or tourists, do come with hopes of a spiritual experience. Notre Dame is many things to many people. Study, teaching, research, sports, residence, family, faith, and Church come to mind. There is something for everyone in such a university that educates the mind and the heart, and which had and has the faith to lift a statue of Mary, Notre Dame, the Mother of God, on a golden dome, and to lift a golden cross on a church steeple reaching to the heavens. We are blessed. This book is a more focused and deliberate effort to cultivate the spiritual life, found and re-found at the University of Notre Dame, and which memory and grace can re-vitalize in this *The Heart of Notre Dame: A Retreat to Remember.*

xii / THE HEART OF NOTRE DAME

Ideas from the classroom, mysteries spoken of and celebrated in chapels, the beauty of the green campus, and memories of life in residence at Notre Dame will all be probed for the deeper meaning now more apparent to us, because we bring the experience of our later lives lived out of those remembrances. We mean to revisit the college years, to recollect the good, the true, and the beautiful. We hope to discover the ways of God by going deeper in our re-membering.

What we were taught back then, thought back then, and concluded back then should be open to a deeper look. "Coming back to Notre Dame" is not about the discarding the past, but more about recognizing its goodness and also the need for change. We have changed. We have learned much by our lived experience. The University has grown along with the times that have made advances in many ways. Our spiritual life may be likened to an old and beloved home in need of some electrical wiring and plumbing improvements according to contemporary code. Not the final word, but a step forward. We may need a dash of humility to live in the discomfort of a spiritual renewal in progress. We may also then find our spiritual home even more dear and lovely to live in. To this end this book is dedicated.

Seven chapters divide this book. Reflections of a page or two are loosely gathered under these headings: Soundings (1), Mysteries (2), Wonders (3), Prayers (4), Scriptures (5), Engagements (6), and Ponderings (7). "Campus" offers an introductory essay, and "Bricks" a concluding essay. Three other essays — The Women,

The Cross, and The Mercy -- come between chapters as a change of pace and a more ample meditation.

When Father Hesburgh retired in 1986, a "Contorted Filbert," popularly called a "walking-stick," was planted in his honor at the Grotto. Twenty plus years later it remains small and covered in an umbrella of large leaves. But, when autumn brings to light the shape of the wildly contorted branches, one finds a surprising beauty in a tree whose only plan must have been in God's eyes. I think of Notre Dame in good times and bad. I think of you and me in our own peculiar contortions, but also our own glory given by God's grace. May you read a chapter of this book at the Grotto and alongside that contorted little tree so easily overlooked.

Finally, you may notice there is some repetition of key insights in the seventy-so chapters below. I had thought to avoid repetition altogether, but these insights are so pivotal that I concluded it might be helpful to repeat them, not in the same words, but with the same understanding, which understanding may not be thought through in its first expression or its first reading.

FOREWORD

A Cautionary Tale
The Whole Truth
and Nothing But The Truth

THE TRUTH IS HARDER to come by than law courts may hope for. The "whole truth and nothing but the truth" may be God's alone. We pursue with difficulty a multiplicity of truths. "What is truth," Pontius Pilate said, and as a governor he was well versed in partisan politics. Truth is always a bit more complicated. I tell my students on the first day of class the following caution: "I do not always say what I mean; I do not always mean what I say, and what you heard is not what I said." Perhaps that disclaimer is an exaggeration, but it should give pause. Pursuit of truth is fraught with the complications of saying and hearing. I also tell my students what window I claim to have on the truth. I am a white, middle-class, American, male, cleric. That's my background and my viewpoint, and I am fully aware that viewpoint is enough to peeve the whole world. My viewpoint, however, is neither worse nor better than another, all things being

equal, but it is limited. Everyone else sees from a limited viewpoint as well, though perhaps not everyone will
recognize his or her own situation. No one knows the
whole truth and nothing but the truth but God alone.
Uniquely God does not observe the truth; God is the
truth. God creates the truth that we discover.

Propaganda, ideology, advocacy, special interests,
advertising, and political rhetoric do not tell the whole
truth and nothing but the truth. Such discourses tell
what is good about their position and what is not good
about their opponent or competitor. What is not good
about their own position and what is good about their
opponent or competitor is passed over in silence. Resu-
més tell what is strong about their authors and overlook
what is weak. Sacramental confession tells our sins but
is silent about our virtues. The whole truth and nothing
but the truth may still elude us.

Post-modernism has urged a "hermeneutics of suspicion." One need not conclude, however, that the pursuit of truth is impossible. One need conclude only that
truth comes with historical baggage and packaged in
language that is opaque. Christianity for many centuries was cozy with slavery in its midst, and today is appalled by slavery. Christianity for many centuries was
cozy with no freedom of religion, and today is appalled
by lack of religious freedom. I like to think such changes were changes to stay the same. The truth of human
dignity was never denied and always acclaimed, but it
was not understood that slave people were human. The
persecution of heretics was thought to be quarantine of
a spiritual "Typhoid Mary," who might infect unto

spiritual death a whole population, but it was not understood that neither the faith that saves nor personal conscience can be compelled.

Human beings can know truth, but in this world not "the whole truth and nothing but the truth." Whether we quote Sacred Scriptures or appeal "to what the Church teaches," or whether we cite empirical science or claim human wisdom, human beings are limited in knowledge and often spin the truth because sin taints us all. That should come as no surprise to those who know our human minds are darkened and our wills are weakened, and that we need the Holy Spirit, given to all people, to illumine our minds and enkindle our hearts. A deep humility befits us all, believer and unbeliever alike, in our pursuit of the "whole truth, and nothing but the truth, so help me God."

THE CAMPUS

An Essay

The movie, "Field of Dreams," imagines that "if you build it, they will come." The campus of Notre Dame is a field of dreams, and they have come from all over the country and all over the world. The campus of Notre Dame covers many acres. There was no need to build upward as in Manhattan or San Francisco. Notre Dame could spread out. The campus is a big field with hundreds of buildings, with parking lots and playing fields, quads with ample lawns, shrubs and trees beyond counting, even forest between the two lakes of Notre Dame. We never outgrow the need to walk through these ancient woods. I imagine some of the trees are older than the university. I know they do not seem to be much bigger than they were when I was a student living at Moreau Seminary on the edge of these woods fifty plus years ago. Oaks grow slowly and live long. They remind me of the essence of education. Wisdom does not come quickly and it lasts as long as we can think.

Walkers, strollers, and joggers circle the lakes and cut through these woods night and day at Notre Dame.

If the trees could talk, how much they must have seen. They know, but they are silent and trustworthy. We need to walk amid these trees, because we need at times to be unobserved and unencumbered. The trees give us privacy; they take no notice of us. The trees of the forest accept our presence without expectations. We need not worry that their feelings will be hurt if we do not regard them. Trees are the most companionable of old friends. They ask nothing of us, and they allow us to be with them in unconditional acceptance that is not lonely when we are surrounded by them towering over us. Sometimes I want to stop and talk to a tree. I think they must be good listeners. Maybe they have even heard it all before. Many of them have been around Notre Dame for a long time, and they have seen it all – students come and gone, secret thoughts and passions brushed over their branches, and laughter rustled in their leaves. A palpable faith in God anchors their roots in mother earth, even as they reach for the heavens above.

The campus is greatly colored by the weather. We tend to complain in South Bend, and we let the heat of August and the cold of February linger longer in our memory than they actually filled our days. So many days on campus are truly beautiful days, astonishing in their lavish display of what generous sun and rain can bring about. Four seasons provide a perennial variety. Springtime excitement and relief merges into lazy hazy summer, and just when one tires of summer heat, a mellow autumn of mildness and fiery leaf color soon follows. Mostly it is winter that troubles the claim that campus weather is not all that bad. What to do with winter in

South Bend? What to do when so often the school year is blanketed with lake effect snow from our mini-ocean, neighoring Lake Michigan. Many of the days through December to April are gray, victims of cloud effect from the same Lake Michigan. Cloudscapes in shades of gray are not without their own beauty. To contemplate the subtle mottling of gray, however, and the constellations of clouds is to discover the chiaroscuro of the heavens. Some professional photographers prefer to work with black and white film to achieve just such profundity. Artists will say that the problem we have is not how to draw, but how to see. We are surrounded with beauty in South Bend, and one of the best lessons learned at Notre Dame may well be to see in the campus, and its people especially, the beauty that the seemingly ordinary reveals to those with eyes to see.

The very young love snow. The not so young, but willing, often join winter and find winter sports. Some folks actually pray for snow. Older folks mumble some about winter snow. Students from the south lament their fate. Nonetheless, let's hear it for winter. Notre Dame students study much harder and bond much better in a blizzard than they might do in a warm and sunny, distractingly and overly busy warmer clime. If necessity is the mother of invention, then trapped in winter is one of the mothers of wisdom. Not always and and not for everyone, but winter can be beautiful.

Our life may well have its own weather. Springtime flowering trees seem just the right background for the campus nubile maidens. Autumn time seems right for the nostalgia of childhood left behind, innocence a bit tarnished, the way things were in rapid change, both beautiful and foreboding. Winter speaks loudest to the moving through middle-age into old-age, calculate the numbers as you wish. The elderly know the fire is going out, much as we feel the sun is waning. I have often thought that the waters of Lake Michigan steer tornados away from Notre Dame. I could not prove it, but tornado alley in Indiana and Michigan does seem to track inland. The isolation of South Bend contributes mightily to the pervasive residentiality of the campus of Notre Dame. The peculiar weather may be providential as well. Such lessons of how God provides and how it is an ill wind that blows no one good are not learned in books.

In Indiana it seems especially fitting to take note of Indian summer. Just when we thought the warm days of autumn were folded into a long winter to come, there arrive a few days of balmy autumn as a brief reprieve. The story is told that the early settlers of the west noted that the native Indians burned off the prairie grass in late autumn with hope of a better spring grass for the buffalo herds. Miles of burning prairie made the air warmer for a few days, and voilà Indian Summer. The story is a good one, and maybe even true.

A large part of the population of the United States lives nearby the Atlantic and the Pacific oceans and the Gulf of Mexico. Human beings evolved along with all life from the sea. We swim unborn in our mother's womb. We seem to be most at home on the shore of a body of water. Notre Dame Du Lac would not be the same without its lakes, which were once upon a time one lake with a marsh between what is now two lakes, connected by a conduit that brings fresh water from the spring-fed St. Joseph's lake to St. Mary's lake, and finally to its discharge at the west end en route to the St. Joseph river. The islands in the campus lakes were formed from dredging to deepen the lakes. Water from Notre Dame flows into the St. Joseph river and thence into Lake Michigan, over Niagara Falls, and eventually into the Atlantic ocean. The north-south continental watershed runs nearby, and Notre Dame waters flow north. French trappers in colonial days came through the south-most bend of the Saint Joseph river (hence the city of South Bend) and with a short portage entered rivers leading to the Mississippi and onward to the Gulf of Mexico.

To what shall we compare the campus of Notre Dame? To an oasis in an urban desert? To a sacred grove long tended by the mandarins of academia? To a Midwest Walden Pond, where students build lofts to rival a homemade cabin and read books while not quite hoeing beans? To the Garden of Eden, a tad past the apple eating and soon to have the gates barred never to be an earthly paradise again? No doubt the beauty of the campus with its trees, bushes, and flowers teach students about the value of nature well tended. God spare the maples from the blight of the American Chestnut and the fungus of the Dutch Elm. What would we do without maple-leaf colors in the autumn sunlight? Perhaps ecology is learned by example at Notre Dame, and to tend the world and its ecological balance is not altogether different than the cultivation and pruning of our campus greenscape. And perhaps we all have more to learn and ways to change in this our stewardship of planet earth.

It is said humankind is never closer to God than in a garden. In Eden in the cool of the evening, God walked with Adam and Eve. It was in a garden that the risen Jesus spoke to Mary Magdalene by her own name, and she then recognized Jesus risen from the dead. The campus is an ample well-tended garden. The balance of wild nature and human boundary finds an equilibrium in this campus garden. Here God and man seem more together. Here nature and design seem more allied. Where else will so young men and women be lords and ladies of the manor and its environs? Campus gardeners, workers, cooks, and maids, all tend the larger garden. Have we died and gone to heaven? With the evergreens by Walsh hall swaying in the moonlight with clouds scudding by with hide and seek peekaboo, the Dome flooded with golden light over one's shoulder in our night, the fireflies in June on the wing, and we might just be in Paradise again. One of the Holy Cross priests who served as President of the university, and who was a life-long poet at Notre Dame, left us a most beloved poem.

> So well I love these woods I half believe
> There is an intimate fellowship we share;
> So many years we breathed the same brave air,
> Kept spring in common, and were one to grieve
> Summer's undoing, saw the fall bereave
> Us both of beauty, together learned to bear
> The weight of winter: – when I go otherwhere –
> An unreturning journey – I would leave
> Some whisper of a song in these old oaks,
> A footfall lingering till some distant summer
> Another singer down these paths may stray –

The destined one a golden future cloaks —
And he may love them, too, this graced newcomer,
And may remember that I passed this way.

Charles O'Donnell, C.S.C.

The Notre Dame campus with its spacious beauty and variety draws visitors and alums alike. "Home-
coming" weekends are named well. As I write today, a
columbaria is being built in Cedar Grove Cemetery
on the campus, because many who loved Notre Dame
want to be buried here. Mobile as we are as a population, the "no place like home" might just be the campus of our yesteryear. Moses in the Exodus story sees
the glory of God in a burning bush in the desert. Perhaps when one is desirous of seeing God, every bush is
a miracle of God's glory. The world may be all-a-glow
for those with eyes to see. I cannot pass the giant syca-
more tree on the fringe of the Grotto and nearby Corby
Hall without thinking here is a sacred tree likely older
than the university itself. The rare earth we walk upon
is but light congealed into matter, full of energy asleep.
Our food is light transformed into the food of our bodies. We are but a wavering light, dim and reflected light,
compared to God who is infinite light. Yet, the campus
is ablaze with light in every growing thing and in every
radiant person made in the image of God. It may not
be a stretch to see the campus as a garden of God's own
making, through our own shaping of it, sometimes more
and sometimes less than we had hoped.

CHAPTER ONE
SOUNDINGS

What We Are Doing

Professor Emil Hoffman taught chemistry to a generation of Notre Dame students who moaned and groaned "eeemil" out the windows of their dorms at midnight before his challenging departmental exams throughout the semester. They carried him in triumph to the final exam in every conveyance they could imagine. Emil was rightly feared and also loved. He taught wisely and graded fairly. First-year students who did well in his class would do well at Notre Dame. Years later along a path from the front steps of the Main Building to the La Fortune Student Center Emil sits in retirement on a bench that should have his name engraved upon it. He talks cordially and wisely to anyone who comes along -- student, faculty, staff, or visitor. He listens to whatever the issue -- the joy or the sorrow. Professor Hoffman reminds us that in the end what matters is not career but care and affection for human beings. What matters is not being all that we want to be in our often imprudent calculation, but being what God wants us to be. And God wants us to be human, only human, fully human. It is a question worth discussing in every classroom at Notre Dame and in every residence hall. What are we doing at

Notre Dame? More pointedly, what am I doing at Notre Dame? I try to answer that below.

WHAT AM I DOING HERE? Why am I here? That is a very good question. And, why anything? Why me? Why am I, when only God is "I am who I am"? And why here, and where is here? Indiana, United States, North America, Planet Earth, Solar System, Milky Way galaxy, one among billions -- we human beings but a speck upon a speck. Here I am lost in space in a world that is nonetheless in God's hands from "in the beginning" to "in the ending." And in the meantime, why am I here? Short answer: I am here to learn to be human. I am here to learn to be human fully, not like an idealized Apollo but like Jesus, who lay down his life for us all. And that is more than enough.

Long answer to why I am here: In the Garden-of-Eden story, Satan's pitch went like this: "Adam and Eve, listen up. You do not want to be human. Being human is a burden. You have to learn everything bit by bit; you have to tend the garden in the heat of the summer; you get bored and you get sick; you will suffer nothing but troubles from lots of others, and then you die. You do not want to be human. You want to be like gods, knowing good and evil, never dying and ever drinking ambrosia from gold cups on white clouds. Trust me! You do not want to be human." Our ancestors should have said: "Get lost; we are here to learn how to be human."

I need to learn how to be my brother's keeper and my sister's too. I do not want to be Cain; I want to be

Abel. I need to learn how to cultivate the garden, how to protect mother earth and build mother church. I need to learn how rare is planet earth and how amazing the tiny miniscules of my body and the immense stars in their trillions expanding at the speed of light, the fastest speed there is. I want to learn to be human. I am here to learn to walk, to talk, to think, to care about a rock, a plant, a dog or cat, and each unique human being. -- each a precious child of God. I am here to learn to care. I am here to be detached from this world, but only after I well learned how to be attached. I am here to learn to care and not to care. I am here to be human. I am here to learn that I must do everything I can and leave everything to God's care. I am here to learn how to spend my life in the discovery that I want nothing so much as to give of myself for the benefit of others. I am here to learn how to be a displaced person, a nomad who has here no abiding city, a pilgrim who knows "this our exile" is a vale of tears. I am here to learn how to await what I know is coming. "Come, Lord Jesus"! I am here to learn how to be human -- how to trust, how to hope, and how to love. I want to learn how to believe wholeheartedly and to love passionately. Even God's Son wanted to become human. Can you imagine – God a baby in a stable who made a woman cry and a man nailed to a cross who thought to say to a stranger crucified aside him in agony: "This day you will be with me in paradise."

I want to learn how to be human. I want to learn how to die, how to go through death with the "bread of life" and not to expect to get a life only after death. I want to want to be born into eternal life when I die and leave the womb of this life. I want to learn to sit at the table and wait until everyone else is seated at the banquet in heaven, for without everyone being happily there I cannot be fully happy. I want to learn to count no lost sheep unworthy of my search and my care, however feeble. I want to learn to want it all and how to wait for God. I want to learn to let go. I want to learn to be human. I want to learn to learn. I want to learn to dance in friendship with God the dance of love, so that when I die I will not be a wall-flower who cannot dance, though oft invited, because, and only because, I have yet to learn the human steps of love. I want to learn how to be human, just that, only that, fully that, human as Jesus was human. I want to learn that only people live forever. That is why I am here. [Previously published in the *Notre Dame Magazine*. Copyright mine]

Wisdom Come with Age, and Maybe Love as Well

The students keep getting younger at Notre Dame. So say their elders. And the students notice their professors are getting older at Notre Dame. White-bearded Father Edward Sorin, C.S.C. and white-haired Father Theodore Hesburgh, C.S.C. remind us both of the vulnerability of us all in aging and the wisdom and love of the spirit abiding in the saints of Notre Dame, even when the human body cannot go on forever. The young tend to be oblivious that their turn will come as well. Age is no respecter of persons. Corby Hall, where the Holy Cross community shares its prayer and its meals, also enjoys the presence of some of the retired and more elderly of its members. I have heard undergraduates teasingly refer to Corby Hall as the morgue, but are they not aware that death comes for us all? A sophomore may have read all of Plato, but he or she surely has not understood it all. Plato knew that the study of philosophy was the study of how to live well in order to die well. Plato knew what our undergraduates can only surmise. Wisdom comes with age, and maybe love as well.

COME BACK TO NOTRE DAME. Come back to when you were young and knew it all, or maybe thought you did. Now that I have come into my senior years, I see so many people, events, and conclusions so very differently. Perhaps we cannot find courage to go on with daily life unless we think we are right and in the know. I thought I knew at least myself. Now I know I never did, though maybe I am closer to the truth in owning the distance from it.

"He who loses his life will find it," Jesus says. Being altruistic, self-giving, and generous seemingly comprises what Jesus means. Yes and no, I think now. Why we are generous and selfless seems to me so often colored by self-interest. People who get along get along so much better. Generosity is admired, rewarded, and trusted. Such a good investment for enlightened self-interest. We think we know ourselves, but only God knows us inside out and from the heart. Only God's grace can overcome our hereditary self-interests. A friend of mine has a German Shepherd dog, which seems to like me greatly. I am one of the sheep she feels responsible to shepherd. She probably would give her life fighting to protect me. She brings a chipmunk that she hunted down and selflessly drops it at my feet as a gift. But, she would not give me a crumb from her well-guarded food bowl, were I dying of hunger. She never learned in her ancestral past how it was in her interest to do so. She does wonderfully what dogs should do, and I whisper in her ear as she rolls over on the rug that it is not easy to be a dog. It is not easy to be a human being either, and only by the grace of

God and in the mystery of the cross may we hope to do so. Becoming human takes time. We need patience with ourselves. "God is not finished with me yet" remains a wise saying. When we are young students we may be either unduly puffed up or undeservedly cast down. Rarely do we know ourselves as we shall know ourselves in our later years. Wisdom does come with age, and maybe love as well, and love of ourselves most of all, from which we are to love others as we love ourselves.

Hobbits and Saints Marching In

The first-year students arrive amid deluge of rains and grass-soaked muddy parking spaces alongside their assigned residence hall. Now it is Sunday and the skies are blue and the sun is warm. Parents, new students, relatives, and friends are all walking leisurely across the campus to the Joyce Center. Thanks to its permanent closing, one no longer needs to cross Juniper Road to reach the basketball auditorium for Sunday mass. I watch them, and I wonder how so much care and love could accumulate in one place. Only the long line of capped and gowned seniors at graduation can compare. It takes many years and a world of effort and patience to raise a child to maturity, and he or she must do a great deal to be selected for entrance to Notre Dame in competition with others talented and blessed as well. Here are the chosen -- all sizes, races, creeds, and color. I cannot help but find them lovely and dear. How God must love them, if even I can see such hidden glory. I cannot help but think of them as Tolkien's "hobbits," vulnerable and fragile little creatures in the great scale of things, but when at their best, the only ones with heart and courage and love stronger than the evil loose in the wide world. "When

10

the saints go marching in" comes to mind when I watch this endless procession across the mighty campus. Children and their parents are streaming to the Lord's table, where there is a plenty for everyone in equal shares. All quarrels and divisions are set aside for the time being in a common love for family and common joy of parents for their children finally at Notre Dame. There remains also a common grief that after this opening mass they are to leave them here, without family of old, in a new and not well known family, alone. They must say goodbye without too much fear or sadness, and then bravely set their face toward home, which will be strangely silent and empty in a way that cannot be described.

ASTRONAUTS SPECULATE about the billions of galaxies, many larger than ours, and each with billions of stars. Surely there are many other planets, other solar systems beyond us and light years away. Some of them could be far beyond us in the evolution of intelligent life itself. One imagines artificial intelligence superior to any brain or any computer known to us. One thinks of artificial life, more complex and invulnerable to breakdown than mortal flesh on earth is heir to. One thinks of super-robots, who can make themselves anew, repair themselves, replicate themselves at will with far more intelligence and technological skill than we ever dreamed of. In such a world, one imagines, there is no human poignancy, no human emotion and feeling, and no love that is filled with wonder and joy precisely because everything in this our world is so fragile. In the

Star-Trek drama, Radar is all but human and far more competent in quick and deep calculations than his human colleagues. He is without human feeling in its fullness. Radar is not quite human, not quite mortal, not quite vulnerable, not quite able to lay down his life for his friends. In Shakespeare's "Tempest," Prospero asks his spritely Ariel if he should finally relent and forgive all of Prospero's unworthy enemies. Ariel replies with a touching awareness of his own lack, even though he is magically gifted to fly through the air and work miracles: "I would, were I human."

God became human in Jesus of Nazareth in order to be one of us. In solidarity he came to share his own life by example of love and by the grace of the Holy Spirit sent into our hearts. I wonder if God wanted to know what it was like to cry with pain and to weep with joy. God knew everything, of course, but did God know in the flesh fragility, vulnerability, and mortality. Jesus is God with us beyond comprehension. In one of André Dubus' short stories, the father of a young girl, who ran over a drunken pedestrian in the dark of a country road, defends his cover up of her accident to his confessor. The priest protests that even God gave up his own son to judgment and even death. The father replies to the priest: "But, God did not have a daughter." With all our flaws we love our children to death, and we send them to Notre Dame because we know they must live their own life. We love them enough to let them go, to let them learn by their mistakes, to let them one way or the other come to lay down their life for those they will come to love.

HOMELESS

The "Homeless Shelter" in South Bend, Indiana came about from the initiative of two Notre Dame professors, David Link, dean of the Notre Dame Law School (in his later years a priest of the diocese of Gary, where he ministers to inmates in the Federal Prison in Michigan City), and Darci Chisholm, long involved with the Center for Social Concerns on the campus. The Bible has a perennial concern for the homeless, for the stranger on the road, for the widow and the orphan without a roof over their head and without resources of their own, dependent on the care of others. Fr. Sorin's love for the minims of Notre Dame, the grammar school residents of early Notre Dame education, included children without much of a home outside of Notre Dame. Today we have on campus many foreign students, far from home, and home that may be full of troubles for them. We have students from broken homes, who are not exactly homeless, but are bereft of the home they wanted. We have students, undergraduate and graduate, who do not know where they will be staying over holidays like Thanksgiving, Christmas, and Easter. "Homeless" may be a temporary condition for many Notre Dame students, but being taken in over holidays by another student's family

13

does seem quite wonderful and one clear instance of the Notre Dame family that would have no one left homeless from their Alma Mater.

MORNING PRAYER in Corby Hall Chapel is a daily event, Monday through Friday, and one of the Holy Cross priests with ineluctable regularity offers the same prayer at the close of Lauds of the Divine Office. For many years each day he makes aloud the same petition: "For our Holy Father and for the homeless." When he is occasionally absent, I am tempted to speak out the same prayer, but I fear it may be seen as more mirth than devotion. And yet, what else is there more urgent to pray for? Are we not one and all homeless on this earth, walking toward our eternal home together in pilgrimage without a lasting city? Does not that walk become easier if one can rest at night with a roof of one's own overhead? Are we not all children of God, yet seemingly orphans in a universe where God is discounted? Were we ever more in need of someone on earth to stand in for our Father in heaven and to speak words of hope to human beings. Our Holy Father in Rome speaks for the pilgrims of eternity everywhere in the world, whether Catholic in allegiance or not. I trust the Holy Father speaks for, prays for, and would help when possible all peoples, for we all are in truth children of our Father in heaven. We are all homeless on earth. We all seek to know someone cares for everyone. Notre Dame, our Mother, brought the love of our Father in heaven down to earth. We may still be homeless, but we are in good company.

Lost Dreams

My brother was thirteen years older than I was. He left home when I was six years old. The only thing I remember of that time was my mother telling him to teach Richard (my middle name) to tie his shoes. Jack did just that, and then he was gone. He was very young when he went off to fly warplanes and earn his wings in the United States Air Force training center in Pensacola, Florida. All the family went there for his wedding, which took place immediately after he earned his wings and before he was assigned to wartime duty. He was young. He had not finished college. The war dragged on and he did not seem to know what to do with himself. He re-enlisted and was sent to Hawaii. For many reasons, most of which I do not know anything about, the marriage broke up. Jack remarried, but he did not have another son or another daughter. He never held one job for very long. Divorce in the Pre-Vatican II days was simply unacceptable amid strict Catholics. We had some in our extended family. Or maybe Jack and Janet imagine they were shunned. He must have felt a failure all round, and I think now that he was a hidden casualty of World War II. He visited home where I was still living prior to *college, and over the years we visited him at times. Then he came down with a fatal cancer. How many lost dreams he must have had, and I recognized at the end of his life a few lost dreams of my own.*

WE ALL HAVE STORIES of lost dreams. We all have lost friends, lovers, and alums. Sometimes there were broken promises, sometime mean words and cruel deeds. Sometimes good people in our life and good aspirations simply drift away or become lost. Tragedy stalks us all in one way or the other. There comes a moment somewhere in the middle of everyone's life, when it becomes clear that our dreams will not all come true. It is either too late for us, or our ideals turned out to be big for us. Either way, we know in our bones that our dreams will be unfulfilled. Human life is a broken one, an unfinished symphony, no matter how well the first notes harmonized. We have here no lasting city. We have no control over other people, events, or most circumstances. We may have written the play we would direct, but the actors take over, and what appears on the world stage is not what we had written and hoped for. What happens in our life, though not what we dreamed and planned, may prove in God's providence surprisingly hopeful.

We are told in the Gospels that those who lose their life will find it. Perhaps those who lose their dreams will find them. Self-surrender is a way into the Paschal Mystery of Jesus Christ. It is a dying that we might come to live. In Baptism we surrender our self-identity and become what we are in truth, God's beloved child. In the Eucharist we surrender our self-sufficiency. In Penance we surrender our self-righteousness. In the Sacrament of Anointing we surrender our self-control. In Ordination we surrender our self-determination, and in Marriage we surrender our self-will. Throughout our life our dreams are not so much lost as they are replaced with a deeper grasp of what the human being in us truly wants and was created to be and to do.

Retired

Retirement used to be mandatory at Notre Dame by age sixty-five. Fr. Hesburgh's presidency was extended five years when he reached that age by a special exemption given by the Board of Trustees. Today there is no legal mandatory retirement, but many Notre Dame faculty retire in their sixties, and if they have been many years at Notre Dame, they retire as millionaires. Prudent savings and investment policies that took a percentage from salary annually and added a percentage from the university in lieu of salary rose year by year, especially in the boom times in the American economy. Professors emeriti continue to contribute to Notre Dame, sometimes as part-time teachers, sometimes with continued writings, sometimes with devotion to former students who return to their teachers for advice or an atta-boy/atta-girl. The Holy Cross Brothers across the highway from the campus have built a village for residential living, assisted living, and primary-care patients. Close to Notre Dame and with the spirit and ministry of the Holy Cross Congregation, many retired Notre Dame people have chosen to live near by each other and the university. Condominiums on the sides of the campus spring up like mush-

rooms around Notre Dame, and many of them become investments for "domers" seeking leisure activity or retirement homes.

PEOPLE IN DANGEROUS occupation may understandably retire after twenty years of some jeopardy. Soldiers and police deserve an early retirement, for the job is dangerous and rigorous. Stress jobs are burn-out jobs. Retirement in its etymological roots tells of pulling back, not necessarily sitting back. Retired people often begin a second career, sometimes work again for pay, often give heart and soul to a volunteer project, or a hobby that one believes in and that one loves. In my own religious Congregation of Holy Cross, we have a policy that no one retires. At age seventy, however, one may choose one's work in ministry, according to preference, ability, and health. One will not be assigned; one can volunteer, and there is always need in the spiritual lives of the people of God.

In retirement I have heard some humorous descriptions that bless such "pulling back." For example, "I don't do anything, and that does not begin until ten in the morning." Or, "I think more and more about less and less." My own contribution goes like this: "I am willing to work, but I do not want a job."

I think philosophy is taught well at Notre Dame. Love of wisdom found a connatural home on this campus. If, as Socrates said, the "unexamined life is not worth living," it would be equally true that the unlived life is not worth examining. A philosophy of life tells us much about how to live, but philosophy at its deepest nature was a study of how to die, how to die well, how to die humanly. And the short answer to that question may well be that one dies well by learning to live well. Retirement is a challenge to turn the page, to begin a new chapter, but not to stop living well before one is asked by the author of life to retire from this world. As we have lived, so we are likely to die.

Old Age

Notre Dame is a university approaching two hundred years of age. Compared to Oxford and Cambridge we are Johnny-come-lately. We believe traditions strengthen over time, and there is no need for Notre Dame to fear the future. And yet we know our own days are limited, and there will be a time when Notre Dame is no more, or at least, not as we imagine it to be today. I came to Notre Dame in 1951 as a freshman, when Fr. Hesburgh was named to succeed Fr. Cavanaugh as president of the university. I joined the Congregation of Holy Cross after residing a semester in Zahm Hall. A new program for college seminarians was housed in Old College, the original building of Notre Dame, built when Fr. Sorin came here in 1842. My life has never been apart since then from Notre Dame, though I taught at the University of Portland, a sister school in Oregon of the Congregation of Holy Cross, and I served as director of novices in Bennington, Vermont, and Cascade, Colorado. I have been part of Notre Dame for the last third of its history. As I write this Fr. Hesburgh is in his nineties and I am in my seventies. Perhaps God wishes Notre Dame to *live forever, though even the stones will erode from wind and rain if enough years go by. We may well hope for the best in the future of Notre Dame, knowing the Lord above and Our Lady have been good to Notre Dame in the years past.*

IN THIS WORLD I would not think that endless life is a blessing, but more likely a tragic destiny. Think of Sysiphus, who rolled the rock to the rim of the mountain top, only to have it escape his grasp and roll back down the hill where he was to push again against a ruthless gravity. To live forever here below is to go around in circles, getting nowhere, perhaps vastly interesting for a time. Forever in this world would eventually be boring - - nothing new under the sun, eventually vanity of vanities, all is vanity. Old age and approaching death from this perspective is a blessing. Eternal life with God is a promise that takes us out of this world to intimacy with God who made this world. Earth is not our home or a lasting city, but remains a passageway to the heart of God, who does not go around in circles getting nowhere. Our life is destined to expand in wisdom and in joy at the end, for which all else we have ever known is but preparation. In our creator is our hidden name. In our savior, Jesus Christ the Lord, is our true love life. In the Holy Spirit is the unimaginable life of God, to which after this our old age we are to be enjoined forever.

And so, shall we not say we do not want to live forever in this world? Shall we even say we want to die? Not maybe so, but surely so. And yet, this world is so lovely at times and so beautiful in places, that life seems truly precious on earth. Even God could not bear to miss its enchantment. Who does not prefer Christmas to Easter? Who does not prefer beginnings to endings, youth in its springtime to age in its autumn? We want to live, now and to come, in this life and in the life forever. I want to die, but not now. I am willing, but I do not volunteer. The only real sadness might be to have lived and not to have been a saint. If this life is a walk with God in space and time, let God lead. Our walk with God would be just right as God chooses, who is our companion, and who came to bring us along with him back to where we began, conceived in the love of the Father of mercies. And Notre Dame will come along in its own way as well.

What God Is Doing

Notre Dame has to be one of the most beautiful campuses in the world. It is spacious with no lack of land. Trees of every kind of beauty flourish in this soil and climate. Two lakes enhance the well-tended grounds with patches of woods and old-growth forest. Plantings of every kind, much like the student body from every place, carry on a tradition of wanting a bit of everywhere to be here and to bloom at Notre Dame. Indiana skies can be blue and bright, and gloomy and dramatic. North and south meet here and clash in shows of delight and despair on the north-south continental watershed. One used to see more stars at night, but ground lighting and city smog have dimmed them except on cold clear winter nights. Sunrises and sunsets can be spectacular, and particularly sunset over St. Mary's lake seen from the Grotto can be breath-taking. Astonishing as the miracle of creation may appear at Notre Dame and all around the world, there is another miracle happening on campus. The transformation of sophomores into seniors, of adolescents into adults, of students into eventual teachers, parents, and caregivers of their parents, rivals the wonders of a material creation.

In many ways, change of heart, what can be rightly called conversion, is the greatest miracle of God. Grace builds on nature, but grace also surpasses nature. What God is doing with us is more awesome than what God is doing with the stars and the stardust that is planet earth. Conversion, baptism, forgiveness: we change. Here is a greater miracle than the creation of the whole world, because God must work with the negative valence of our sins and the true freedom of our wills. In creation, nothingness did not talk back. Cain did talk back in the hardness of his heart's freedom: "Am I my brother's keeper?" The miracle is that we change. God does not change from angry to merciful. We change from hard-hearted and unloving to soft-hearted and compassionate.

Religion is about what God is doing, and very much less about what we are doing. Worship is at the heart of religion, much more than ethics, though behavior is important and follows any change of heart. God has no need to change from infinite love. It is we who change, and that change is all about what God is doing within us, around us, and for us. God, who created us his children and created us out of nothing, continues to save us from ourselves in his goodness and mercy that follows us all our days.

Love is Strong as Death

If you have ever lived on a campus with young people who come with love given them in the past, you cannot but notice how good they are and how much such loved people love others in return. The saying that "hurt people hurt people" is balanced by "loved people love people." Notre Dame students have been and are much loved, and they respond with much love and idealism. Their behavior is not always good, but their heart more often than not is in the right place. Bad judgment and a failure to "think about it" accounts for much that goes wrong in residence life at Notre Dame. Throw in some alcohol and you have the perfect storm. However, Notre Dame students astonish us veterans with their persistent creativity for good, their initiative at home and abroad for helping the needy, their invention and generosity in undertaking what is new and seemingly impossible. The Center for Social Concerns at Notre Dame is the hub for much of this kind of activity beyond the campus, and daily care of one another in residence hall gives rise to the belief that love is common as grass. We take in good people at Notre Dame; we pray that we turn them out even better.

What makes the world go round? Perhaps chance events, perhaps evolutionary advantage, perhaps the creator and divine providence, perhaps in our despair the blind force in "a tale told by an idiot and full of sound and fury." In our faith and hope it remains the "love that moves the sun and stars," as Dante concluded. If love makes the world go round, we live in a very lovely world. The Bible's short collection of love poems has long intrigued religious sensibilities. Read as a cycle of mystical love poems, the "Song of Songs" speaks of the courtship of God and Israel, God and Church, God and the human soul. The world is a love story; human life is a love story. At the close of the "Song" one line may linger in one's memory: "Strong as death is love" (8:6). Most people think they know what this line means. Love survives death. Love is forever. "Till death do us part" is not exactly the hope of those who believe in life everlasting. "Till death do us unite" is the hope of those who do not believe the grave is our human dead end. Love is forever, and the beloved walks with us together to the God who is love and whose love makes the world go round. But that is not what "strong as death is love" in the Bible means, true as such an eternal love might be with trust in God's promises.

Here is the meaning of "strong as death is love." Death pursues everyone in this world, and though one can postpone death, one never outrun death. It captures everyone in the end. But, the "Song of Songs" promises that love is just as resourceful, just as persistent, just as perduring as death. Love also pursues everyone

in this world, and though one can postpone its blessing, one can never outrun love. Love captures everyone
in the end, because "love is strong as death." God is infinitely resourceful and pursues each one of us through
the hills and dales of our lives. "If God is for us, who
can be against us"? (Rm 8: 32) "Strong as death is love"
(Sg 8:6).

Real Presence

If wisdom is to be sought, known, and defended any-where in the world, in these our days it would be in a uni-versity, and very likely in the Department of Philosophy and in the Department of Theology. Surely this is the situation on the campus of Notre Dame. All undergrad-uate students are required to take courses in philosophy and in theology, because Notre Dame stands or falls on the claim that are truths of reason and there are truths of faith. Sophism in the ancient world, nominalism in the medieval world, and historicism in the postmodern world are not unrelated. The human mind has always been plagued with doubts that issue in skepticism, relativ-ism, or cynicism. Do we know anything beyond our own knowing? Is knowledge just words, manipulated in end-less ways and some of them quite fascinating, or do we ever make contact with real presences and know some-thing beside knowing ourselves? What we make of the world with our minds and express with our words – per-haps useful knowledge that even allows us to manipulate nature – need not be the truth and nothing but the truth?

There is no Truth (capital letter T) is the bane of the intellectual life and a constant temptation for intellectuals at a university, who know how much of all knowing must be subjective, even if such subjectivity does not preclude the pursuit of some objectivity. The "view from nowhere" of empirical science may need to accommodate the "view from here," which is the scientist's own contribution. Is anything in the end present besides our own words? Are there real presences and can we know them, however imperfectly? Every university student will encounter this question in one way or the other, and every human being presumes something about the truth and its pursuit. We are all to a large degree products of our education.

We talk in Christian faith of a real presence, but the present to our mind is a strange real. The future is not yet, and our future moments are never guaranteed. The past, our life for what it is worth, is all in the mind of God and with bits and pieces lodged precariously in our minds as well. The present is real, but gone into the past faster than I can write it down. The present is real like the river flowing by. Only in God does the present, the past, and the future all coalesce in the eternal now, when "a thousand years are as a day, and a day as a thousand years" (2 Pt 3:8).

There are also real presences, realities that precede our mind and our language. We come to know something or someone when we come to love someone or something. We do not know or love only our words. Our language constructs the real presences, but it does not create them. Words arrange our mind and color our emotions, but the real presence of real things and real people turn us on and demand our attention, which is but shaped and amplified by our words in their elaborate beauty and confusion. Now you know, my Romeo, Juliet is not just a play of words. "Crying is a puzzler," Darwin once said. A love to die for and a faith to die for is a puzzler too.

THE WOMEN

An Essay

WERE I WRITING from St. Mary's College next door to Notre Dame, I suppose I would entitle this essay, "The Men." The pros and cons of coed education have never left an easy conclusion in my mind. There may be no conclusion that is a resolution. You gain and you lose by same-sex education; you gain and you lose by co-ed education. Some gains may show one's preferences; some losses may reveal one's priorities in life. The women at Notre Dame, however, was not an issue of the value of coed education at all. Then what was the admission of women students to Notre Dame in 1972 all about? Women at Notre Dame was about not changing Notre Dame, or more exactly, it was about changing in order to stay the same. The University of Notre Dame was founded to provide a quality Catholic-inspired education for the future leaders of American society. Because doctors, lawyers, politicians, business men (sic), journalists et al. were in overwhelming majority men, the university educated men. When it became clear, thanks be to God, that women were well on their way to be-

33

coming equally leaders of society in the traditional careers previously closed to them, Notre Dame should educate women. It was not a choice as much as a change in order to stay the same. One might argue that a Notre Dame should have been an engine for changing society to admit women to the workplace instead of the caboose on the train of culture change. One might argue that homemakers and mothers benefit themselves and their family by a quality education. Perhaps so, though to educate someone at a university to assume responsibilities that would not be there for them may not have been all that helpful. Universities may at times lead culture change, but more often as an institution they must adjust to it.

Change to stay the same may not have been a coed issue, but rather a human issue of the leadership preparation for the future of society. Dormitory living at Notre Dame suggests that coed education as a philosophy of education does not overwhelm single-sex education. Enrollment at Notre Dame is coeducational; residence halls at Notre Dame remain single-sex dorms. Are there pros and cons? Of course there are. Does one's choice of all-male and all-female residence hall reveal some priorities at Notre Dame? Very much so, I think. Bonding in a residence hall is hard enough without issues of privacy and rivalries that a coed dorm may well create. No doubt some coed dorms in some places provide a positive living space. Perhaps some day Notre Dame will initiate some or all coed dorms. However, I would not hold my breath in anticipation. The richness of single-sex dorm life has been long tested at Notre Dame, which has long been a close-knit residential campus. Life for students at Notre Dame has thought to provide a home with minimal complications and with rich rewards. Men and women at Notre Dame cross paths and become part of each other's lives in so many other ways than a shared dormitory when it is time to call it a day.

That women wanted to play sports so avidly, when adequately funded and encouraged, did surprise me. I was not surprised, however, that women at Notre Dame excelled in academic pursuits. Some would say they outdo men on average in competition for admission and in grades achieved in the classroom. I suppose one could crunch the numbers, but numbers are not the whole story. Ten years beyond college the intelligence of students may prove somewhat more even. Male students may be more rambunctious in their college years and less willing to use their potential for study. Women students may be more willing to do academic work as asked of them and then find limitations of gender lingering in the workplace. I do know that women have brought a woman's touch to campus, a woman's perspective to learning, a woman's way all around all the time. Notre Dame has been enriched by their presence beyond measure. I am not sure I could tell you how a woman thinks that is demonstrably different than a man. I am not sure I could tell you how a good Catholic novelist differs from a good novelist who is not Catholic. In the reading of the best writers I do pick up a tone, a perspective, a valuation that is always subtle but very dearly appreciated. I pick up that same subtlety in women's ways, including ways of thinking, ways of caring, perspectives, tone, and an appreciation of what most needs insight and care that often seems most rooted in heart and personal identity. Men do this too, I know. Boundaries are fluid. Nonetheless, unless one is color blind, one knows there are shadings of the palette that always bring surprise and joy.

Reminders of the Holocaust seem to come in a never-ending stream — lest we forget. The Jewish community can hardly forget what they suffered, and an effort to keep the memory alive accounts for books, films, memorials, and anniversaries. Christians do much the same in their Sunday masses. "Do this in memory of me" makes the mass a memorial of the cross of Jesus, then, now, and forever. When I catch a glimpse of the many ways over many centuries that many millions of women were deprived of protection, of education, of opportunity, I am overwhelmed with shame and guilt. Anger arises, even from self-interest, as one recognizes all the gifts of mind, body, spirit, and soul squandered or left undeveloped, and to the detriment of victim and oppressor alike. All minorities suffer in much the same way, but women are half of the human race. There is much to lament. It may help also to claim than many men loved many wives, daughters and held in high regard women in general. It may help to claim that I did not deprive women on my watch, nor enslave blacks, and so forth. It does not help very much. Our Lady's University should hold a special destiny for women, which is buried in its roots and proclaimed on high in gold. I do not expect to live to see that destiny fulfilled, but I yearn for it and I believe in it. "While her loyal daughters go marching on to victory" may never become the fight-song lyrics, but such new song may be the hymn of life in a better future for Notre Dame and its women.

Edgar Allan Poe thought there was nothing more poignant than the untimely death of a beautiful woman (see "To Helen"). The life-giving potential of the feminine may be the explanation or it may be the sudden collapse of great beauty -- the beautiful without which we cannot live. We have lost young men at Notre Dame, but I most remember the bus accident that took the lives of young women, and the car crash on the way to their western home that took the lives of two sisters in one family at Notre Dame. Prof. Catherine La Cugna's funeral at Notre Dame still gives me pause. She was too young to die; her spirit and mind too beautiful to perish so soon.

Mary Cassatt paints in one of her pictures a woman seated at the opera in a box seat with a mirror on the wall behind her. She is strikingly dressed and attractive in her setting. Going to the opera is about the music and theatre, but it is also about the display of human beauty. This young woman seems in bloom like a flowering tree in spring. She will turn heads. The women at Notre Dame have brought soul to campus, mind to classroom, and also young life-giving beauty to our campus. You do not have to plant flowers on a campus, but once you have seen what joy they bring the human heart, you would sorely miss them. God bless the women of Notre Dame. God bless the men of Notre Dame as well. God bless us all, young and old, figured and disfigured, all of us beautiful in our humanity for those with eyes to behold a deeper beauty.

CHAPTER TWO
MYSTERIES

The Problem of Evil

*The Notre Dame residence halls are not built for priva-
cy. Students share common spaces, including bathrooms
and study rooms. Roommates are assigned in the first
year, and not always guaranteed in subsequent years.
There has to be a lot of acceptance, and there is plenty
on campus. School life is not always sweetness and light.
School bullies, whether with force on the playgrounds or
with slander on the Internet have made cruelty among
the young not unheard of. Date rape can happen. Innocence can be ruined in college years by the pressures of
so-called friends. Sex and violence on TV and film per-
meate our culture. Violence especially seems to ratchet up
with the latest explicit abomination broadcast. Raise the
stakes and we find in real life everything from torture to
the deliberate exploitation of innocent persons even unto
death.*

EVIL SEEMS AT TIMES so obvious. Surely the Holocaust
qualifies. And yet the evil of it all was so banal. We have
photographs of Nazi concentration-camp officers en-
joying a perfectly bourgeois picnic in the lovely country-
side and listening to soul-touching music from the great

German array of classical composers. When I watch the ever-growing wild violence on our television and movie screens, I think it must be the triumph of evil. And yet, it seems to be shrugged off by younger generations. I cannot bear to watch violence, and I cannot swallow jalepeno peppers in my Mexican forays into such cuisine. Others do not find the food hot at all, nor the violence a soul-shuddering evil. Perhaps one becomes callous in an effort at self-protection. Accordingly, more and more pepper or more and more violence is needed to stay even with the current. Drawing and quartering the human body is hard to imagine and seems an unspeakable evil from past centuries. Crucifixion as punishment of an even earlier time might seem terribly evil as well.

Why is there evil in the world? "Deliver us from evil," (or from the evil one) concludes the Lord's Prayer. Demons would at least take the banality out of evil. Whatever one concludes, surely evil is real and one ignores it at one's peril.

Four explanations for evil can be given. (1) An evil God or demi-god, opposed to God, is at work. (2) No one is in charge of the world and evil just happens. (3) A good God is in charge, but helpless in face of the abuse of human freedom, which God has given to human beings. (4) A good God is in charge of even human freedom. Evil is a great mystery, and good in the end will triumph over evil, even though our ways are not God's ways.

The devil talks to God in the *Book of Job* and makes

a bargain. Take away from Job family, possessions, and even his health, and see if Job does not curse God. Job laments, but he does not curse God. The devil in *Faust* talks to him and makes a bargain. I will give you women and power over the world in exchange for your soul. The implication is that no one will choose God over worlds of evil-gotten goods.

I conclude that evil remains a great mystery. Jesus overcame darkness on the cross of Calvary. Of human suffering and the evils of sin he gave no verbal explanation, but he did show he would walk through the suffering of evil with us. The whole world and all who are in it will come to know their moment on Calvary. People of faith in the God who made the world of nothing, and whose providence is sovereign over all, know that evil is real, but impotent in the end, for God the Father almighty has no equal. If human nature indeed is intended to bend toward the good, the seeming triumph of evil is truly absurd. But even absurdity has been embraced and defeated by the God-made-man on the cross and by his glorious resurrection.

Brave New World

Notre Dame students are plugged in, or wireless, but very up to date. Land phones are no longer in the rooms. Cell phones pervade the airwaves and replace wrist watches, and onward. One can email a student or call them long distance on a cell phone number that may not be easy to obtain. Utube, Facebook, Blackberry, Ipods, Google, Wikipedia --Games and Letters and Photos – you can have it all, like it or not, on a small device in your hand as you walk along the paths of the campus, ear plugs in place, and sometimes eyes locked on a screen rather than a scene. We have gone digital in a big way on this campus, and perhaps it is all for the good. It is not my world, and why should I make the bed for these brave young students who should lie in the bed that they make. To me it looks a bit like their unmade bed, or a bed in progress, but then I worry too much about the future, as old folks are wont to do. I worry about the freedoms of the USA, the character of UND, the survival of CSC, the welfare of the UN, and the health of the VATICAN. The only one thing I never worry about is whether God forever loves us all as made manifest in Jesus Christ. I know only people live forever, and when the lights went out one evening past in the graduate student housing where I then lived, we talked to each other at length. It seemed like a wonderful world of neighbors you could touch even in the dark. Virtual reality may be coming, but I miss actual reality if it is going. I know guns do not kill people, only people kill people, but let us not let a teenager drink and drive. Sometimes we do think about consequences. Birth control may be reasonable, but lots of girls and boys do not seem to be reasonable, and human life does not seem quite so prized world-wide. Is this progress? Maybe, and maybe a brave new world.

SOME WISE MAN quipped that if one is not a liberal when young, one has no heart, and if one is not a conservative when old, one has no head. Liberals strive for freedoms; they are empathetic with suffering and observant of injustices. They are often right, even when the implementation of what they urge is dead wrong. The truth may be that human beings cannot handle many freedoms. They need to be saved from themselves, say the conservatives, although to monitor other people's freedom is always a temptation to control them and abuse their God-given autonomy. Nonetheless, anyone who has seen freedom, given an inch, take a mile, or seen a good cause championed turn into a riot without any responsibility, know that conservatives have a case to monitor human freedom. It used to be kegs-on-campus was the issue. Then hard liquor on campus was an issue. Both issues lost out, as does the issue of co-ed dormitories, though the question never goes away. We ought to be free to buy prescription drugs, buyer beware, but we know we lack both knowledge and discipline, and we need to be saved from ourselves. Broken hearts and trivialized sexual lives are predictable outcomes, and yet we do not know quite what to appeal to as a remedy for too much sex, too soon, and too casually.

The best example of Martial Law for the sake of the common good is underage drinking. We don't call it that, and it is not well enforced, but wartime is what it is about. How can a young man or woman obtain a driver's license or a pilot's license at age sixteen or so and not buy a beer? How can one vote at age eighteen and not enter a bar? How can one fight in a war with weapons of mass destruction at age eighteen and not throw back a bud? Sad experience gives the answer to this conundrum that seems so hypocritical to teenagers. Underage drinking and driving turns highways into killing fields. It need not be so; some teenagers, no doubt, could drink and drive carefully. But, way too many cannot figure it out. If they drink and drive they maim and kill themselves and everyone else of whatever age in their path. In a war it would be called collateral damage. In peacetime, society declares Martial Law and imposes a curfew on teenagers, who are legal and free to drive, but will not be legal and free to drink until both brain and judgment have matured enough to allow them to handle a four-wheeled gun. Adults do not do much better, sad to say. "Brave new world" where marvels of technology may not be without their problems for everyone.

To ponder these matters is to face what they offer to, and take away from, children and grandchildren. It isn't possible for things to revert to simpler times. Perhaps the best we can do is to model and coach those in our care in the ways of civility and the need for quiet, uninterrupted space in which to think. Talk there must be – perhaps we can help provide our charges with something worthwhile to say.

Brothers and Sisters,
Is There a God?

The existence of God and the immortality of the soul are the two perennial questions in philosophy and in religious studies. If there is no God, we are orphans in the universe, seemingly but specks upon a speck in a vast and cold and violent cosmos. If there is no immortality of the soul, then death is a dead end that is the end of us. Nothing of our lives may seem quite so poignant without hope in God and hope in life everlasting. I never met an atheist in my life as a college teacher and as a priest. I did meet quite a few people who said they did not believe in God, but when I asked them to tell me what God was like, whom they did not believe in, I had to agree with them. If that is what God is, then I also do not believe. In the main, atheists are made by bad arguments for God, bad explanations of God, and bad behavior on the part of those who claim to believe in God. There may be real atheists out there, but I have never met one. Everyone believes in something. Everyone has doubts. Perhaps those who believe are right, or perhaps those who do not believe are right. Sometimes humanity seems certain of only one thing. We know we cannot know, and that conclusion seems a bit self-contradictory on the face of it. A world of injustice and cruelty does not seem to deserve a God, and much of the anger about the existence of God is anger about the suffering God does not dissolve. Disbelief is a way of getting even. Overall, we have considerable diversity in matters of belief at the University of Notre Dame. What is especially good, however, about Notre Dame remains just this. One can talk about God at any time or any place and not be considered weird. That is not always true elsewhere.

EVEN THOUGH WE WERE created in God's image, we return the favor and create God in our own image. Almost always our God is too small. An infinite God is not easily thought about, and a finite God is hardly worth thinking about. It is hard to decide which behavior fosters disbelief in God the most. Would it be the sinful behavior of those who claim God exists but live as if God did not? Or, would it be the bad arguments for God's existence on the part of well-intentioned believers, whose God is too small. I am not sure I know the best argument for belief in God. No one argument has ever convinced every well-educated and well-intentioned person. The Catholic Church maintains human nature is capable of reasoning to the existence of God, but it does not cite who has done so and with what argument.

Where one begins in a discussion of God's existence makes all the difference, I want to say. If I decide to start with myself and ask where is God, it is probable what I will conclude. If I decide to start with the mystery of it all and ask where am I, and why am I, it is also probable what I will conclude. Belief understood as trust in God is a very personal question. We are not so much asking can you prove the existence of God is a fact or a proposition that might leave the intellectually challenged among us at a loss. The question of God is more like this. Will you trust yourself to God? Yes or no. The question of God is more like this. Will you marry me? One cannot answer "I do not know" or "I am not sure." Such responses are a "no," at least a "no" for now, with maybe a "yes" to come at a later date. Will you trust me allows only yes or no, as does the question will you marry me. Follow someone around for a day; see if they kick the dog. You may discover what they do not and cannot say, what they really believe about the good, the true, and the beautiful. Those who claim not to believe should not despair. Who knows what non-verbal belief may dwell in their heart, even unbeknownst to them? Those who claim to believe and say all the right words should not be presumptuous. Who knows what non-verbal disbelief may dwell in their heart, even unbeknownst to them? Talk is cheap. Walk the walk and talk the talk are not the same thing. Show me, don't tell me. Live what one believes, and believe what one lives. In the end, only God knows, God knows.

Sign of the Cross

In college years at a university that draws from far and wide one learns that not everyone does things the way they were done at home. Right and wrong become elastic, and study abroad, now so common at Notre Dame, just stretches the point. Our understanding of life and how to live it may not be the only one, nor the best one, nor one without need of change. Education at its best must be a broadening experience. When we were very young we needed to be taught right and wrong quickly and without much qualification or nuance. Do not cross the street. Ever. As we grow older we recognize that one may cross a street with care and prudence. Children are not ready to make distinctions. Much of our early religious education was geared for children. Memorize, take my word for it, do not probe until you are older. There are many ways that children are indoctrinated, because at an early age they can only gradually be educated. In the meantime, they must live. We do not raise a child to be a citizen of no country until they are old enough to chose a nation they admire. They will be raised Americans by the culture, and its values will most likely be reinforced by home and school. When one arrives at college away from home it may feel like higher education is a demolition of home-won truths. Perhaps one does need to have the wiring and the plumbing brought up to code, and new windows to give a wider viewpoint, but in the meantime when childhood presumptions are being undone, and more critical and insightful conclusions are under construction, one is uncomfortable living in a tent in the backyard. Such are college years.

AT MORNING PRAYER today I made the sign of the cross with my left hand. Perhaps I made it backwards. I do not know, but it was so liberating to recognize that it does not matter. I meant no irreverence. There is nothing wrong with left hands, nor crossing shoulders right to left or left to right. We were taught the right way, and perhaps as a child I assumed it was the only way. Right hand and then to left shoulder and then right shoulder. Easier done than said. Orthodox Christians sign from right shoulder to left. But surely it does not matter. To make the sign of the cross is a matter of heart and not of geometry. Coming back to what we were taught as children can free us from those constraints of childhood that needed defined boundaries, precise instructions that allowed no deviations. To travel the world is to discover in space that people do the same things, and live and die, in so many different ways. To travel down memory lane is to discover in time that we need not all choose the same life or give an account of our values in the same way. Just because our many teachers had no time to speak of further insights does not mean we

need to stay in childhood explanations. Coming back to
Notre Dame may well be a review of more than the sign
of the cross.

Fundamentalism

Visitors to the campus often need a map to make their way. There are so many buildings, xxx and counting, and even alums returning to campus can be puzzled. Try to find your way to the Hesburgh Library or the Snite Museum in the most recent embodiment of campus roadways. There remain the map-makers and their products available at the Visitors' Center, and there remain those who walk the campus and know the terrain from experience. Graduates returning to the campus may well discover that what they were taught is not always and everywhere still being taught, at least not in the same way and not with the same arguments.

MAPS NEED TO BE REVISED. Truth does not change, but truth does develop. We discover more of truth; we correct errors in our perception of truth. We learn how to embody the truth in words that are more winged words that fly to the heart of the matter. We change, and to mature is to have changed often. We learn from our mistakes. We have confidence that we might be right today, because we recognize some of the ways we were wrong yesterday. We suspect the re-visioning is not over with

today, and we want sometimes change in order not to
change in essentials.

Revision of maps a time ago was not a simple matter.
There was no satellite photography. Maps were drawn
according to the remembrance of the explorers of virgin territory. Once maps were made and spread about, a
certain presumption arose that the maps told it the way
it was. Were a traveler to come back and say they know
the terrain on foot and the map is wrong, they would
have to overcome fundamentalism. The map-text is
presumed right,whatever modification lived experience
might suggest. Since experiences differ, the master text
of a Bible or the antiquity of a map does give warrant to
hold to the past. And yet, maps change.

Reading the Bible is not an easy art. The texts are
ancient. We would be puzzled by a newspaper two or
three thousand years old. The cartoons, were there any,
would puzzle us. The language would baffle us and a
culture of long ago even more. Reading today's news-
papers is no less complex than reading the Bible, but
we are tuned in. We know the most truth in the daily paper might be found in the obituaries, though even
there the cause of death may be fudged. We are suspi-
cious of advertisements; we recognize spin in editorials;
we know news stories were written with a deadline. We
know if the Cougars destroyed the Lions, there was no
blood on the sports field. We catch humor and irony in
comics and cartoons with some ease. We know how to
switch gears, to identify different kinds of writing in a

daily newspaper. We are not so able when we read the Bible and want to take it all word for word as a reasonable facsimile of an eye-witness videotape. Fundamentalism as a reading strategy is so simple, accessible to everyone, demanding of no long study, giving certitude seemingly. Such reading does not depend on insight that might be rare and nuance that might be subtle. Yet, it does not account for the fullness of the truth.

Fundamentalism in ethics or moral theology holds for a consistent right and wrong. Circumstances may aggravate or alleviate, but the end never justifies the means. What is wrong is always and everywhere wrong. The truth may not, however, be that simple. For centuries the world endured slavery, and even the Church, from St. Paul to the Catholic bishops of colonial Maryland, found slavery somehow acceptable. One could not imagine the world without the benefits of slave labor, and hence what was inevitable must somehow be acceptable. We no longer hold human slavery to be a moral option. Human slavery can even be characterized as intrinsically evil. Our moral theology had a blind spot that finally was overcome in the nineteenth century by the inspiration and efforts of evangelicals more than by mainstream religion. We should be grateful. We now have learned how all human beings are equal before God and cannot be exploited, given their dignity as a child of God. What was right yesterday is wrong today. It may be as simple as that.

The acceptance of religious freedom at the Second

Vatican Council gives an example of what was wrong yesterday is right today. There was a time when the Church proclaimed that error had no rights, and that heretics were subject to punishment even unto death, because they were dangerous to the unity of the State and dangerous to the eternal salvation of those people whom they would lead astray. We hold freedom of conscience now and that without exception.

In the end the problem with fundamentalism is the demand for certitude rather than the desire for insight. Fundamentalism seems a safe place, which is why we fall into it, but our hope is in God whose ways are not our ways. Our trust is in God who gives us the Holy Spirit. To grow is to change and to be mature is to have changed often. Maps are helpful, but maps must be revised. Those who walk the terrain, map in hand, may well know more than the maps of yesteryear can tell.

Silence Without Noise

I do not live in the downtown of a big city. I live on a rural campus in a small city. Notre Dame should be quiet. More and more it succumbs to noise. Some of it we do to ourselves with earphones chanting perpetual music or cell phones broadcasting conversation on every walkway. We used to have reel mowers with a pleasant whirl. Now we have the SUVs of the mowing world with an engine adapted from a light tank. They come by the dorms in early morning and by the classrooms in the late morning. We have garbage trucks that hoist huge metal bins over their heads, shake them like a dog shakes a rat, drop them to cement with a clang, digest them with an accelerated grind, and then roar off to the next bin with the squeal of tires, air brakes, and the engine from a heavy tank. Window air-conditioners moan, and construction and repair trucks wind up every imaginable hydraulic device. Rug cleaners come with enormous vacuum machines that whine on by the hour in the evening, early or late, when the carpet traffic is light. At night volunteer bands of drummers and bag-pipers wander the inner campus lest we forget noise. Silence seems intolerable. Having had my say, let me now claim that our students, with all

*the noise that their education generates, remain the rea-
son why Notre Dame is here, alive and well, though now-
adays a bit more noisy than it ought to be.*

NOISE CROWDS OUT SILENCE as weeds crowd out flowers.
There is no end to weeds, because a weed turns out to be
whatever does not belong where something else is cultivated for beauty or for food. Noise is the weed of the
sound world. It pops up, or blasts out, most everywhere.
Lakes that once knew row boats and sail boats now are
drowned in the roar of jet-skis that whine in circles of
spray and in one's face. There is no way one can broadcast silence. One can never take noise away with silence
imposed on others, but noise imposed on others always
takes away silence.

Come dawn, quiet can be almost complete, as it seems
noise must eventually sleep as well. One can find some
silence around the campus lakes and amid the tall trees
in the dell of ancient woods on the path along St. Joseph's lake to the Calvary cross at the hilltop end of the
outdoor Stations of the Cross. Those trees do not speak
or take you into account. They do not expect you to talk
to them or to listen to their story, though you can do
so quietly. They broadcast only silence. Moments of silence, without trucks, machines, airplanes overhead, or
sirens in the distance do occur at times. There are moments. On a New Year's day, the university being closed,
I walked the whole of the paths around the God Quad
as a gentle snow fell. There were only my footprints and

there was no noise of any kind. People make noise, but there were no people but me, and my footfall was muffled by the blanket of deep and soft new-fallen snow. Silence is a plenum, and I imagine God living in an infinite silence that contains every word that could ever be spoken and then some. A white page, like a white snowfall, waits with infinite expectation for the first black scratch on its surface. Until one writes this and not that, the white page of silence stands in for the infinity of God, who contains all that is and all that could be. Eternal rest may be heaven's promise, but I hope there is no eternal noise before the face of God where a silence that is golden may well prevail.

No Away No Way

For a number of years Notre Dame disposed of its detritus from residence halls with large dumpsters that a giant Waste Management truck would pick up regularly at some most inconvenient hour. The campus puts out a lot of junk waste. Paper and plastic make up the most of what accumulates room by room in the residence halls and classrooms. Cost per pickup led to installing compacters of our own, which reduced the number of dumpsters greatly. In the end, however, there still is no solution to throwing things away because there is no away. Unless we send our garbage on a rocket to the sun, it would still be there and in our life somehow somewhere, because there finally just is no away. If we burn garbage we must breathe it in some form. If we bury garbage we will be drinking it in some form sooner or later. Some waste can be recycled by nature's own waste management, but so many chemicals and metals of a technological society never go away. Atomic waste is only an extreme case of a long-lasting and very harmful waste product. The

communion of saints is a doctrine that claims that any-
thing any one of us does for good or for bad will impact
to a degree all of us. We are one body of Christ, and it
would seem that we are also one body in the global cam-
pus that is planet earth, where anything we manage, for
good or for bad, impacts sooner or later all of us.

INSIGHTFUL MOMENTS leave cascading implications.
"Nothing is destroyed," suggests we can only change this
material world, but not take out of it anything we seemingly destroy. We can burn a forest, but the trees become gases and eventually the gases will become trees
gain. The "conservation of energy" has long astonished
me, just as liquid water, ice, and steam seem miraculous.
"There is no away," is another such insight. One cannot
throw anything away because there is no away no way.
You can bury trash, send detritus into the oceans, sail
ozone into the stratosphere — it is all still there somewhere in our soil, our water, our air — our rare and fragile planet earth.

"Nothing is lost," is also a psychological insight.
Whatever we have thought, felt, or done, leaves a trace
somewhere in body or in soul. It is all there, perhaps forgotten and irretrievable, but never erased. Even com-
puters hang on to what they know. Erased from the
screen and normal access, the data is still hidden there.
We worry about forgetting hard-earned knowledge, fond
memories, basic names for things and for people. God,
however, forgets nothing, retains all our letters and

scrapbooks, loses no memories, seeks all our treasures and is not inclined to be a garbage collector.

"Nothing is in vain," is yet another insight. "All things work together for good for those who love God" (Rm 8: 28). In the heart of Tolkien's *Lord of the Rings*, we can find hints of a providence: Things are meant. There are signs. The heart speaks. There is a way. Whatever belongs to a life will enter, and whatever enters a life belongs. God writes straight with crooked lines. The providence of God provides for everything, and chance events are but the mysterious ways of God we have yet to comprehend. Jesus appears after the resurrection with all the wounds of his crucifixion. Our scars go with us into heaven. Our history with its heartaches is never lost, but only trans- figured into glorious wounds. Not a drop of pain is wast- ed. Nothing is left behind. All will be reclaimed, recy- cled, renewed, saved and brought with us in the creation of the new heaven and the new earth that will last for- ever. "There is no away," is good news. There is no de- struction, only transformation. There is no lost that is not found. There is no in vain. We believe in the resur- rection of the body, memories and wounds alike, and life everlasting. We believe that God who created this vast world "in the beginning" from nothing will recreate this new world "in the ending" from everything. Even sin will serve, for there is no kingdom of evil that escapes the sovereign providence and love of a God who loves not what is sought out for good but makes good what God chooses to love in creating and creates in loving.

How God Knows the Future

Present-day students at Notre Dame have too many choices. They are so talented that many careers are open to them, and many paths beckon. The "road not taken" looms ever larger, and the outcome is often one of indecision and unwillingness to risk a commitment, much like the donkey paralyzed between the bale of hay and the bucket of water, unable to decide if more hungry or more thirsty. Of course, we do not know the future. As the joke goes: Question: How do you make God laugh? Answer: Tell God your plans for the future. We are not guaranteed the next second. Dante thought this earthly life was a Divine Comedy, because despite its awful sufferings it was a story with a happy ending and a wedding banquet in heaven. From what we can see at hand, however, many lives and many empires appear to be tragedies, which end with failure and death because of unavoidable flaws, careless mistakes, and personal sins. Jesus in his humanity also did not know the future. One might surmise that he was as surprised with the resurrection as the disciples were. "My God, my God, why have you abandoned me" (Mk 15: 34) does not foreshadow a divine comedy and its happy ending. Our choices in school or in life remain wrapped in mystery.

ONE MIGHT CLAIM RIGHTLY that religion is about what God is doing, and not primarily about what we are doing. Religion is about worship in the main, rather than about ethics, though ethics is always important in the pursuit of true human fulfillment, both our own and others around us. Saints are truly happy; sinners, regardless of exterior façade, are truly unhappy. Nonetheless, we adore God alone who is doing everything in us, with us, and for us. God provides creatively for our path to him, pursues and captures us all, and guarantees that all things work together for good for those who love God -- and one might add, for those whom God loves. And God is love. Thus a mighty hope can be born and sustained in us all for the future of us all.

How does God provide? How does God know the future? Does God influence slightly or mightily, or not at all, the future events of our lives in this world? One way to understand how God knows the future and what divine providence entails for human freedom is to negate the image of God as a spectator awaiting future events. Parents are spectators waiting what their children will do with their developing freedom in years to come. Scientists are spectators when an errant space probe escapes their control only to eventually descend to earth unpredictably from a disintegrating orbit over which they no longer exercise control. God is not such a creator on the sidelines, wringing his hands, hoping for the best from errant humanity gone astray and capable of fostering most any atrocious outcome. The "spiritual" that sings of God's providence should be taken without compromise: "He's got the whole world in his hands." That kind of providence not only knows the future but makes the future, and in so making it, knows it. That providence is not waiting to see what happens. That providence knows what will happen because nothing has existence in its being or in its activity but that the hand of God has touched its core and given whatever life there may be to whatever there may be. God's providence thus is not God seeing the future, like a spectator learning something new from seeing something about to become actuality from many possibilities. God is not waiting to see what happens, and coming to know it before we human beings do, because of God's higher vantage point. God knows the future not as one learning from events or projecting outcomes from abundant information and shrewd premises. God knows the future because God is creating the future as an artisan makes an artifact.

We need to think more expansively of God in God's infinity and eternity. God is not a member of any category or a species of any genus, not even of "being" itself. God is not one more being, albeit the biggest being. God is not well spoken of as infinite being. God is existence itself beyond the category of being. God is not an essence, a noun, however great. God remains pure act, a verb, whose existence is his essence and whose essence is his existence. God is all one, simple and undivided, whose truth is his existence and whose existence is truth itself, and goodness, and beauty, and all the ninety-nine names of God. Such a God we know but "in a mirror dimly" (1 Cor 13:12), and by analogy with our created world, known feebly by our created minds trying to comprehend with human words the uncreated infinity and eternity of God.

God is not one more person in the room, but invisible and bigger. God is not one more player in world history, but incognito and stronger. *Time* magazine gives a section to religion, as if alongside of science, politics, entertainment, human interest, etc., God is also a factor in the history of our times. God is not a player in history; all the players in history are in God. God is not in the future; the future is in God. God does not learn the future; the future is known by God in creating the future. Such is the mystery of God.

Beyond Miracle

One of my colleagues asked his theology class at Notre Dame what might be their "heart's desire." He was fishing for a deep-sea answer concerning the ultimate meaning of human life. One student claimed his heart's desire was a red sports car. The question had been misunderstood. There are things we desire, but there is also desire for the spiritual. As children we may have wished upon a star. I have often thought if I were given one wish regardless of what it might be, I would wish for a thousand more wishes. Then I would get to work for myself and others. Not much better than the red car, I fear. What might be the heart's desire of the human race? Surely a university should explore that question. What is the one wish that is unsurpassable? That the infinite God would become a tiny child born for us, and who would live among us with compassion and die for the love of us and the preservation of our life, seems to me that greater than which nothing else can be imagined. Improbable and outrageous as such a desire may be for God to become one of us in irrevocable and gratuitous love, that serendipity is what Christians believe to be the truth of Jesus Christ.

WHETHER TRUTH IS WHAT human beings make, or what God made and we discover, exercises philosophical argument with regularity. Whether miracles happen or events we cannot explain generate miraculous explanation exercise theological argument with regularity. Our faith, however, claims far more than any miracle can deliver, and the truth is beyond what any human mind could discover. Revelations is just that. What we could not claim, we hold as true. Let me explore the greater-than-life as we know it with some examples.

Jesus of Nazareth is God incarnate. Mary of Nazareth is the mother of the Son of God made flesh. The one and only God, infinite in all categories because beyond all categories, unique and eternal, almighty God, became a tiny child that made a woman cry. We are not talking now about a miracle. Jesus is not explained by a claim he is a fatherless child, a virginal conception, an exception in nature that we cannot yet explain, a miracle of God's power that believers might claim. Jesus may be all that but much more. No miracle can produce the incarnation of the divine. Adam claims no human father, and Adam is not divine like Jesus. Incarnation of the Word of God made flesh is awesome mystery of another plane of existence altogether beyond miracles that exceed natural causes. Awesome and unfathomable, impossible to our logic and reasonable mind, beyond imagination, that God could be so small and, moreover, would choose to be small for our sake makes the Christmas crib scene a boundless wonder and awe.

One thinks that the greatest of miracles might be the raising of the dead. Jesus raises from the funeral procession the only son of the widow from Nain. Jesus raises Lazarus, whom he loves, the brother of Martha and Mary, even though it was four days after his entombment. We must, however, never think of the resurrection of Jesus from the tomb and from death as such a miraculous return to this life. Lazarus will die again. He is not resurrected from the dead unto eternal life. Lazarus is resuscitated from the dead with a return to mortal earthly life. Resurrection of the dead as Christians understand it remains beyond miracle. No one has a claim on eternal life but God. No one has a claim to see God face to face. No one has a claim to enjoy God's love forever. It is a great mystery beyond all miracle.

There is no videotape account of the resurrection of Jesus. No one knows the when or how. The tomb is empty, not to let Jesus out, who walks through the stone as he walks through the closed doors of the upper room where the frightened disciples will hide. The tomb is empty to let the women in to see that Jesus is not here, but only the burial cloths neatly rolled up. Resurrection is more than miracle in our world. Resurrection of the body surpasses time and becomes as an event in eternity. The body of Jesus is not in the grave, but our remains will not be anywhere else. God does not need a dead body to resuscitate. Resurrection of the body and life everlasting is a new creation for a new heaven and a new earth. Such a creation surpasses miracle as the

21

original creation from nothing surpasses all our imagination and understanding. God's ways are not our ways,
and God is truly beyond miracle.

Trinity Mystery

There is a crucifix in every classroom at Notre Dame, and one as well in most every public room on this campus. "Lift high the cross." Nothing at Notre Dame is higher in the heavens than the golden cross atop the steeple of the Basilica of the Sacred Heart. We believe in the sign of the cross. "Hail the cross, our only hope" remains the emblematic words of the Congregation of Holy Cross, the founders and sustainers of the deep religious impulse of the University of Notre Dame. We cross our selves at times in the day with the sign of the cross, and the words we say are the same words we say when we baptize "in the name of the Father, and of the Son, and of the Holy Spirit." If we prize the cross so much and trace the sign of the cross upon ourselves so often, what do we think we are doing? How do we talk of the Father, the Son, and the Holy Spirit. The hardest day of the year to find a volunteer homilist at mass is most surely Trinity Sunday. Of this great mystery we seem to be tongue-tied. And yet, who God is remains at the heart of all religion, and Christ on the Cross is the revelation of God. "Who sees me sees the Father" (Jn 14:9) by the grace given us by the Holy Spirit.

ONE OF THE MOST SAD funeral processions from Sacred Heart Basilica to Cedar Grove Cemetery at the entrance to Notre Dame took the body of Catherine La Cugna to her resting place on earth. She was a theology professor at Notre Dame and a young theologian whose insightful book on the Trinity, *God With Us*, promised much to come from her before her untimely death. She wanted us to understand the Trinity not in philosophical terms that could hardly be understood, but in the saving acts of God for us that could be experienced. I like to think she would find her own writings in what I want now to say about the Trinity.

In the Father we see the gift of everything that is the gift of creation. We have someone to give thanks to and we are not orphans in a cosmos where we just happened to be found. We were given life by a Father, and the world was given life as a gift of love of the blessed Trinity, which love is most fittingly appropriated to the Father from whom all blessings come. In the only begotten Son of God, the gift became self-gift -- "my beloved Son, in whom I am well pleased." It is the voice of the Father that Jesus of Nazareth hears at his baptism and again at his transfiguration on Mount Tabor. Gifts of an infinite God can be lavish and enormous but without cost. Giving us the self-gift of God in giving us his Son, God has given us everything. We had no claim to existence in our creation, and much less had we a claim to the love of God in the self-gift of God in Jesus Christ.

So great is the love of God that the Father would have us not fail in the acceptance of his love. God gives the gift of love and the reception of that love to every human being in the outpouring of the Holy Spirit. By grace of the Holy Spirit our minds are illumined and our hearts enkindled to receive the love of God. How God does all this for everyone is the at the very heart of the mystery of the sovereign and infinite God. We do know that no one is left out of God's love, and that the Holy Spirit enlivens everyone.

God is infinitely resourceful, and just as we should not be presumptuous of God's mercy so we should never despair of God's overwhelming providential care of each one of us. In the creation the Father created the world from nothing, for the infinite God is everything, and it is seemingly impossible to our logic for something to be anything if God remains everything. But so creation was "in the beginning." We are not God, and yet we are within God, and yet we are creatures outside while inside of God. In Jesus Christ we believe that God will create the Kingdom of God as a new heaven and a new earth, not now created out of nothing, but created out of everything, good and bad – even sin serving a sovereign God. Nothing will be lost, no tear shed in vain, no joy or sorrow without its being part of the finished picture. In the gift of the Holy Spirit who dwells in us as in a Temple, God has given a guaranteed reception of his own gifts. Our conversion from sin and hardness of heart is a creation from less than nothing. Only God

could create from less than nothing, from a negative valence that is sin, and despite a recalcitrant human freedom that remains true freedom before God. In our
conversion to God, whether known or unknown to us,
whether put in words or never spoken at all, we find the
greatest miracle beyond miracles, the creation beyond
all creations, the ineluctable grace of God that is the
love of God shed upon us in the outpouring of the Holy
Spirit.

The Christmas Crib

So many Christmas-crib sets differ. I am not sure I have ever seen a duplicate. The Nativity scene at the Grotto on the Notre Dame campus is life-size, and I see parents bringing children to see it. I still prefer the miniature sets. Even the intermediate size in the Lady Chapel of the Basilica at Notre Dame, which seems right for the church architecture, seems wrong for me. I stare at the small crib in Corby Hall chapel and I think why God might have loved us and became so small. Human beings in our behavior are not always loveable, and indeed one can easily drift over to Jonathan Swift's position in Gulliver's Travels. Accordingly, human beings are not as reliable as horses. They are no damn good in their cruelty and greed. Still, God must have seen something in us that we might be missing. Of course, God's love was not so much drawn by our goodness as giving us our goodness. We are made good by God's love rather than drawing God's love by what we have done. And yet, there is something about humanity that must have attracted God. I stare at the miniature crib set during the Christmas season and I ponder the question. There are the sheep, the camels, the oxen, and the ass, and there we are. Quite a zoo. What's so special about us? Could it be our need and our misery?

TOLKIEN IN HIS MASTERFUL trilogy writes about hobbits, who are a shorthand for human beings. They are loveable but not flawless. Most of all they are fragile and vulnerable, and yet capable of great devotion and persevering courage way beyond what they can muster in size or power. Hobbits seem to be common, taken for granted, just plain cute, but underneath the appearances they own a good spirit and a full heart. Human beings, just like hobbits, are a curious blend of boundless spirit and bounded body. Spirit and matter would not seem readily to go together so interestingly. Like water and oil, they are never quite reconciled.

Back to the crib. So God said I do not choose to become an angel, held above all that stable dirt, and I do not choose to become the cosmos, above all the angelic host who are but a part of my creation. I choose to become a baby boy. How about that! I stare at the crib. So what would I do if I had God-like powers to become whatever I wanted to be. Suppose I could reincarnate myself, but as what. Lions are king, whales are big, eagles can soar, antelopes can run, cats are clever, and dogs are loyal. Dogs are devoted to their human family. They will lick the hand that feeds them, and even the hand that beats them. They hold no grudge; they are always happy to see you and want only to be with you. I swear dogs are trying to talk, and they surely understand words. I think they think they should sit on a chair and take their place at the table, for surely they are almost human. So I look again at the crib and think to myself. God chose to become a human lamb; Jesus was the Lamb of God. Why a lamb? I never have had any dealings with a lamb, but I know they are meek and gentle of heart. Like the hobbits, they are fragile and vulnerable. They depend on the shepherd for good pasture and water, for protection from marauders. Their devotion and total faith in the shepherd is simply given without question. They are easy prey, and they are the animal of sacrifice. Unlike the dog, sheep have no history of the wolf in their blood. I stare at the crib. The Son of God loved us so much he became a baby in the manger, where the straw was put for the animals to eat. He became the Lamb of God. He became the bread of life. He became one of us, like to us in all things but sin. Jesus became altogether devoted to us, and even hanging on the cross at the final end of the Christmas story, he spoke well of one of us at our criminal worst: "This day you shall be with me in paradise" -- that last great measure of devotion. Like our birth that we did not deserve, so our death may turn out to be a blessing we also did not deserve.

No Triage In God

Nothing is more important for a rector in a Notre Dame residence hall than this advice. Learn the name of everyone of your residents as soon as possible. There is nothing that can do more good, and there is no substitute for recognizing someone by name. Town and family come as a bonus when possible. The Great Banquet in the Gospel tells of compelling everyone to come to the feast, for no one is expendable and everyone missing will truly be missed. We are included not because we are good, but because God is good. We are invited by our need, not by our virtue. There is no one self-sufficient and no one hopeless. There are only people in need of mercy. God has no orphan children. No one is unimportant. On the campus no one should be nameless, and no one should feel they do not belong. No one should not be seen, valued, and cherished. If abortion and euthanasia are held in disrepute at a Catholic university it stems from the irreducible value of every human person, however young or however old.

AT AN ACCIDENT SCENE, medical emergency rescuers must decide whom to help first. Not everyone can be treated adequately at the same time. No sense in treating those who, no matter what can be done, are going to die of massive injury (pain medicine, of course). No need for emergency treatment for those whose injuries will be survived without emergency treatment (pain medicine, of course). But, let us treat those for whom timely and sufficient emergency aid can save their lives.

One can equally imagine triage in a banquet invitation list. Those who will support our cause no matter what place at the table we give them can be ignored. Those who will not support us no matter how high a place at table we give them can be forgotten. Those who can be swayed or manipulated by high place at table should be courted, and our invitations become calculations, a kind of triage in the accident scene that is politics.

God is not into triage under any circumstance. None of us are self-sufficient and can survive without God's help. None of us are hopeless and beyond God's help, however grievous our wounds. All of us are led to green pastures by the Good Shepherd, who lays down his life to protect and save his sheep. God will do whatever surpasses all our ideas of calculation. God will leave the ninety-nine and seek the one lost sheep in trouble and danger of death, for everyone is uniquely precious in God's eyes. With God no one is left behind or left out, and God's infinite resourcefulness is never exhausted. He knows us all by name and calls us in a voice we recognize, however long that may take. We have, therefore, every reason to be a people of hopefulness, always and everywhere and at all times.

CHAPTER THREE
WONDERS

The Enchantment of the World

What are we going to do today? Surely that is a common question. As work demands grow, no doubt those days take on a trajectory of their own. Still, every day has choices. What shall we do with out time? Students on the campus have no need to make a living or hold a job of any major consequence. At no other time in life do students have such disposable time. Classes take up but a few hours of sixteen-hour days that require no making a living, cooking a meal, or cleaning up. What shall we do today? Let's go for a walk, and we'll talk. How many times have we said this to someone? In my time at Notre Dame, how many times have I walked around the lakes, usually only the one, but sometimes both on a gorgeous Indiana day or early in the morning on a muggy summer day. Do you know that a fairly active person who walks three miles a day, as is easily done moving around an ample campus such as Notre Dame, will walk around the earth at the equator every twenty-five years? With a long life one might circumscribe the globe three times at the equator on foot, which not even Magellan boasted of. No wonder we complain of tired feet. Three months trek-

king across Africa, and five months walking across the Pacific Ocean, and onwards.

SUPPOSE WE WERE to offer you a trip no travel bureau ever dreamed of. Suppose we would do today and every day what can hardly be imagined. We would take a walk with God in time and space. Our life would become a journey, and God would be our companion in the world God created out of nothing. No astronaut could ask for more. We would touch down on Planet Earth in the Milky Way Galaxy, and we would find ourselves strangely at home in a vast universe. No adventure could have more suspense or better companionship. God walked with Adam and Eve in the garden in the cool of the evening, and Enoch was seen no more. Alas, we are not in Eden, even though the beautiful oasis-campus of Notre Dame in northern Indiana seems a reasonable facsimile. Nonetheless, we walk with God and every day. What shall we do today, God said to me. Let us take a stroll on Planet Earth created for you to roam. And then one day I came up with courage to say to God. Let us take a journey in time and space together over a lifetime, walking side-by-side and talking of our life and loves. Let us walk the walk and talk the talk on this speck of earth within a tiny solar system in a huge galaxy amid a billion galaxies around it. And God said that was exactly what he had in mind. No wonder we have tired feet, a dazzled mind, and a heart overwhelmed with gratitude. And God said, "Let us go on together forever."

Dewfall Nostalgia

This morning I took my early morning coffee and sat down on my favorite bench by the Sorin Letter Inscription opposite the statue of Saint Joseph on the sidewalk leading to the Old College and the Log Chapel at Notre Dame. It was my late mother's birthday, and she would be one hundred and thirteen years old were she on earth. She is alive, but missing in action, as it were. She is with God, and I believe she knows I remembered her birthday. I seem to forget so much now, but then I remember her birthday more keenly than when she was alive – scratch that – than when she walked this earth. There I sat on a bench somewhat damp from the sprinklers that pop up God knows when. The grass was green. Could we have lived with orange grass? Blue, maybe, and with a yellow sky in the Van Gogh manner, or maybe the golden skies of heaven painted by the icon masters of long ago. We are blessed, and only repetition dulls the glory.

THE DEW WAS ON THE GRASS this morning, each drop a perfect diamond on every blade of grass. God numbers the stars and counts every hair on our head. God is feeding us all, just as every blade of grass is bedewed.

Lucretius and Democritus thought an infinite number of atoms over an infinite time could account for dewfall and a bench at Notre Dame. Some physicists today think that an infinite number of universes can account for the delicate life-supporting balance of planet earth, a rare environment in the known universe. A monkey throwing up infinite alphabets for infinite chances may eventually at astronomical odds leave us the complete plays of Shakespeare. But, why anything at all? Why not nothing? No universe at all. Nothing. And could God create the dewfall out of nothing? What else could account for existence? Seems wonderful to me, and more plausible than the monkey business.

The Sacred Quadrant

At Notre Dame when I was teaching full-time, I thought education came down to this. Learn to know what you know and what you do not know, and learn how to learn. A turning point in the philosophical and theological education of college students seemed to me this. Do you recognize the same questions coming up time and again, though always in a different guise? The wisdom questions are un-resolvable mysteries for human logic and mere words. We know more than we can say, and we raise questions for which the answer is not given in this world. The world is God's world, and God's mind far exceeds our mind. We approach wisdom and we do recognize when the truth is not well served, but in the end we may have to kneel in admiration rather than boast of our comprehension of the final truth.

THE CIRCLE, THE TRIANGLE, and the square have fascinated not only geometry students but mystics as well. Four-square covers the commonsense dimensions of the world. East, west, north and south; right, left, up and down; fire, earth, air, and water. Human beings ask one question of their lives all the time in one way or the other, and there are four possible answers to this one compelling question. Is there truth to be known and consequently loved?

The question of truth and the love that follows upon it depends on your point of view, where you stand, and what window forms your perspective. All knowledge is a view from somewhere. God's knowing creates what is there, and God's view is the view from everywhere, indeed an infinite everywhere. Empirical sciences from ancient to modern times strive to approach in so far as possible the view from nowhere, the pure objectivity of scientific truth and human reason, provable to everyone everywhere. Each of us has a view from here, a view that is real but a view that is mine alone. Subjectivity may be relative to each person, but each person and each view is part of what is there, what is objectively there, and as real as any other object of our knowing. The hesitant, the agnostic, and the skeptic, whether called sophists of antiquity, nominalists of the Middle Ages, or post-modernists challenging all foundations in our own era, they all claim a certain relativity of time and place. There is no indisputable presence; there are only words. What we know most is language. What we see is the view from there – someone else's mind, some historical era, some tradition, some hidden presuppositions that color everything, some beginning point un-confessedly assumed, some unrecognized prejudice that impacts everything seen and said thereafter. There is some truth in such caution, for the human mind is limited, and the human heart is not disinterested in its own particular spin of the truth. We come to truth in a community rooted in revelation(s).

What we perceive or notice remains only a fraction of what's what. There is more going on than we are aware of. Musicians hear more and better what sounds do abound. Artists see more and better. What's what is a profound question. Did I see the arrow on the logo of the Fed-Ex truck? "What arrow," I said? I looked at Fed-Ex trucks for weeks, and I saw no arrow. No shaft with feathers, which was my image of the arrow to be found, appeared. One day I saw the very large and stubby arrow on the painted side of the Fed-Ex truck. That arrow was absolutely obvious, yet never seen by me, and now it remains an arrow I can never not see. It jumps out at me. Until that moment of discovery or insight, however, I did not see any arrow. I did not connect the dots. I did not imagine what was what. Viewpoint and perspective, what you see and what is what, remains at the bottom of our endless philosophical quandaries. Faith and reason, religion and science, truth and opinion, God's Word and our words — all our antinomies pivot on the question of point of view. In the Beatific Vision we hope to share God's point of view, the view of all mysteries from absolutely everywhere.

How Does God Do It All

How do students on campus do it all? That would be my question before asking about God doing it all. There may have been a time at Notre Dame when students asked what there was to do around here. The university now has come a long way. Lectures on every topic, entertainment with music, theatre, and sports abound. No one can do it all on campus these days, or even a good fraction of what is offered and would prove worthwhile. Calendars are full, and electronic devices manage, and sometimes add, to a complexity hardly imagined a few years ago.

SOMEONE ASKED ME a question I had never given thought to before. How does God think of and attend to everyone at the same time? And I then added to that question in my puzzlement: And how can God be everywhere at the same time? Here is what may well be the cause of confusion in such complexity. As we noted above (see "How God Knows the Future"), we often think of God as one more person in the world, albeit bigger and more powerful. But, God is not in the world, nor in our lives; the world and our lives are in God. God is not one more player in history. All history and all its players are in God. One then might ask, does God know the future? The answer, in so far as we can propose, is this. God is not waiting to see what we will do, nor having a sneak preview from a higher vantage point. God is creating the future at every moment and the future is in God, not God in the future. That exactly is the problem. God is everything and we are someone. Creation itself is out-side of God, but then how can one be outside the infi-nite. If God is everything, how can anything be some-thing? But, here we are. We are not a piece of God. And yet we are within God, and that is to our minds God's problem. However shall God manage to create a person-al bond with us? What must God do to be a friend to a human being? The incarnation of God in Jesus Christ need not be inevitable, even if it be a remedy for our sin-ful separation from God. But, it seems to me that the

human Jesus was the perfect bridge from God to us and from us to God. Matter separates us all and all things into endless number of pieces, but God is simply one and everything. That simplicity, which holds all of us within it, is how in the deep realms of mystery God knows all things, reaches into all places, permeates all times, keeps track of all of us, and loves and speaks to each one of us.

Does God Suffer?

When Notre Dame is the first university a student has ever attended or the first university at which a new faculty member has taught, there is a temptation to lament this or that condition on campus. At times expectations for Notre Dame are thoroughly unrealistic. This campus is not perfect. Sin is an equal opportunity employer. Nonetheless, when you have not seen life elsewhere in all its glory and all its debility, you may not recognize how blessed one remains to study and to teach at Notre Dame. We have a beautiful campus, a talented and caring faculty, students who bring the treasures of love and devotion poured out upon them, and a few who without much help from others found the resources within themselves to make a life. Our Lady's University may well have a special grace. I know it has been a special place for the last fifty-seven years of my life, and I have attended two other universities and taught at another one.

IF COPERNICUS AND GALLILEO dethroned planet earth as the center and hub of the universe, it was Darwin who destablized the living world of planet earth. Mother nature became "red in tooth and claw." Life on earth had now to be understood as the survival of the fittest, and everyone was eating at the expense of the life of someone else. Why such a world of suffering and destruction? Would not a wise and beneficent creator have better provided for his creatures? Why not a different world? Why not a better world, according to our lights?

The compassionate Buddha has seemed to millions of people the embodiment of a thoughtful response to this world of suffering. Jesus of Nazareth is not recorded laughing, but he was known to weep over Jerusalem and its pending destruction. He wept for his friend Lazarus in the grave, and he told the widow of Nain not to weep at the funeral of her only son, whom Jesus intended to raise from the dead in compassion for her. So, we perhaps cannot avoid a very germane question. Does God suffer? Does the suffering of our world and our bodies impact the happiness of the Almighty creator of heaven and earth?

Does God suffer? Short answer: yes and no, or in other words, no simple answer. On the one hand we want God to feel our pain and to have compassion for us, as we do for others whose pain touches us, and which we share to some degreee as if the pain were our own. On the other hand, we do not want to burden those we love with our troubles, and we look for that day when we will share with God that eternal life that is precisely not subject to change, to loss, and to pain, but is infinitely, eternally, and securely happy once and for all.

Jesus does weep when they show him the tomb of his friend Lazarus. His compassion and pain prompt him to raise Lazarus from the dead. He tells the women of Jerusalem not to weep for him on the way to Calvary, but for themselves, whose destruction Jesus foresees in his compassion for them. Jesus surely suffered, and Jesus is God. Hence we can say God died for us in compassion for us on the cross. God suffered because Jesus, who is Lord, suffered. But, it is the human Jesus who suffers, though we truly can say God suffers.

God in heaven, however, does not suffer. God dwells in endless bliss, untouchable by anything negative or painful that we or anyone else could inflict upon the Almighty, who holds all existent beings in the palm of his hands. We do not hold God in our hands dependent. God is never in our power; we are always in God's creative power. And we should rejoice that God is invulnerable. If we could hurt God, grieve God, bring pain to God, than the following situation would obtain. Generous and good as God might be, our bad behavior would burden God and makes it harder to claim that God's love for us is unconditional. No matter what we do, God's love for us is never diminished. Suppose we were to avoid bad behavior and relieve a suffering God, would that not impact a love thought to be unconditional? How could it not be under those circumstances? Precisely because God is not vulnerable to our sins do we have a blessed assurance that God's love for us is truly unconditional, gratuitous, serendipitous, irrevocable, unsurpassable, and finally touchingly incarnate in the flesh of Jesus, the Son of God made flesh, who could suffer and who was crucified for love of us.

Given Time and Space

Notre Dame students are most generous with their time, and time is treasure. To give of your time is to give of your life. Business people point out that time is money. We know we have only so many minutes given us. They may be numerous overall and they may not be. Each moment is precious. The young men and women of Notre Dame volunteer for dozens of charitable programs around about to help others in need. After graduation about a tenth of our seniors give a year or more to service of the common good in some capacity. Where one gives time may be more revealing than where one gives money. The Center for Social Concerns began very small at Notre Dame, but looms large now in every in-coming class.

TIME SEEMS TO GO FASTER as we age, perhaps because a day or a week is an ever-smaller fraction of a lifetime. Einstein's theories tell us that time is a dimension and that its speed depends on our speed in space, which turns out to be curved and not straight. We are *a* center of the universe, though *not* the center of the universe, and yet we are but a speck upon a planet that is a speck in an awesome and mega-gigantic universe.

Time is a gift of God. The moments that flow on like a river do have a beginning, and they will have an end. Time is a creation of God, whose moment is an eternal one encompassing every moment and every possible moment however astronomical the creation. We have time to spend, and we spend it sometimes foolishly and sometimes lavishly. It is estimated that we spend three months of a lifetime opening junk mail, on the basis of a few minutes day after day. Brushing one's teeth and checking email must add up to months as well.

"What is time" puzzled philosophers from the pre-Socratics to Augustine and beyond. What time is it? Sounds like a simple question, and with atomic clocks and quartz watches we think we know the answer. But the moment that is now is more mysterious. By the time your request for "now" is heard and a response given, it is no longer the now that one asked about when saying "what time is it"? That time is always past and always coming. One will never capture now, yet we live only in the now.

Space is equally a gift of God. "Where am I" seems as profound a question as "What time is it?" In these foundational questions into the mystery of life where one begins may well determine where one will end. I could begin by saying I am here, and where is God who begs explanation and justification? Or, I could say God is here and where am I, who beg explanation and justification to exist at all?

Perhaps I am making Anselm's argument for God as "that which nothing greater can be thought," and surely to exist is better than not to exist. My less philosophical argument for a world of time and space that comes loaded with questions would be this. Imagine a world where squirrels yearned for acorns but there were no oak trees. We might find that world absurd. If human beings yearn for the meaning of time and space and claim a world of meaning because there is hope of love and life after death, and they were to live in a world without foundation for any of all that, would not our world be absurd? Of course, the world could be absurd, one might say in response. But then, what would be the point of my writing anything or you reading anything. We might merely be amusing ourselves, I suppose, but would not the dead silence then carry all the meaning.

THE CROSS

An Essay

THE CROSS AT NOTRE DAME cannot be missed. The gold cross on top of the Basilica steeple is taller than the statue of Mary on the Dome or the top floor of the Hesburgh Library. "Lift high the cross" prevails in the campus policy that no building shall be lifted higher than the cross, which Father Sorin with much faith, hope, and daring placed on the steeple of a campus church more expansive and expensive than Notre Dame could afford or then needed even remotely. The cross was simply our "only hope" (spes unica), the chosen motto of the founder of the Congregation of Holy Cross that founded Notre Dame. You will find many crosses on the gables of the 19th century campus buildings. The Main Building, once the entire university for its main purposes, is dotted with roof-line crosses. Most every public room, especially student classrooms, display a crucifix somewhere on the wall. The mystery of Jesus on the cross cannot be avoided at Notre Dame.

Most young people encounter the mystery of the cross dramatically in the death of a parent, a relative, or a friend. Less dramatically, I think, students recognize the cross in the limitations that impinge upon them. Intelligent mind, attractive body, and virtuous soul are in large part the hand we were dealt by our birth and early years of formation by others, as well as by ourselves. The news of the day reminds everyone that we live in a world, whose current hand of cards we also must hold. We can play our cards well or badly, but we are trapped or blessed or something in between by where and when we find ourselves in the world. In short, our powerlessness and vulnerability, our very human creature-hood experience imagined in a thousand ways, speaks of the cross. Jesus was nailed to his cross and could not move away. In youth there will come a moment when we know what is done cannot be undone, and what is is and will remain. We know the cross whether we ever heard its name or not.

The words of Jesus on the cross differ in the gospels. Mark (and Matthew repeating Mark) seems so dark. "My God, my God, why have you forsaken me" (Mk 15:34). John, however, seems so light. "Mother here is your son; son here is your mother" (Jn 19:27). Luke gives both the light and shadow of the cross. "Father forgive them for they know not what they do . . . This day you will be with me in paradise . . . Father, into your hands I commend my spirit" (Lk 23: 34-46 *passim*).

Another reading of Judas may make more sense of what we ponder. Along with the other disciples of Jesus,

Judas wanted a Messiah who would be the long-awaited king and who would liberate Israel from its oppres-
sors in the Roman Empire's occupation. After all, Jesus
could walk on water, raise the dead, calm the storms,
make bread and win out of next to nothing. He surely
could lead a revolution to free Israel. All that was needed was to light a fire under his feet. Were he arrested, he
would have to break out of prison and that spark would
inflame a following and a new day for Israel would follow its Messiah. The presumed plan of Judas then went
horribly wrong, much like a practical joke that unintentionally kills someone. Judas in his own crucifixion
knows only despair. Jesus was never supposed to suffer
and die. He returns the money and he hangs himself.

There is some Judas in all of us. He did indeed
betray Jesus by a willful manipulation of him. He wanted to change the vocation of Jesus that came from God.
Peter had tried the same tactic when Jesus predicted his
passion on the way to Jerusalem. Peter protested such a
finale, and Jesus scolded the prince of the Apostles with
harsh words: "Get behind me, Satan" (Mt 16:23). Peter
goes on to deny Jesus three times when he sees the help-
lessness of Jesus imprisoned. We carry our own cross
like Peter, like Judas, for we also are inclined to manipulate others according to our own plans. We cause great
harm in our misconceived, ignorant, and actually self-
ish attempts to make things go the way we would have
them. Jesus would have said to Judas, had he hoped for
forgiveness, "Father, forgive [him], he knows not what
he does" (Lk 23:34).

Recall the situation described in the popular song, "Tie a yellow ribbon round the old oak tree." The husband has just been released from a long prison sentence. In preparation for his return to the world at large, he writes a letter to his wife, whom he has harmed by his foolish ways and the troubles of his life that troubles her and their whole family. He asks her to tie a yellow ribbon around the old oak tree in the front yard of their home, should there remain any love in her for him, all undeserving as he surely is. When he takes the bus along their road he will know not to get off at his home, if there is no yellow ribbon. He finds the oak tree with many yellow ribbons, and that tree may well stand as the cross of Jesus, the tree of life and hope, which delivers us from the imprisonment of our sins and restores us to our home with God. Divine love continues to love us all, undeserving as we be. The cross is our welcome home from the prison of this life's lovelessness. We are loved by God always, and when we allow the yellow ribbon and the tree of the cross to touch our hearts, we become loving persons who no longer need desperately to strike out in all directions. God's love is faithful, and the cross is a yellow ribbon we wear around our necks and tie up on the walls of our rooms.

The cross means many things to many people. To some the cross gives value to suffering as redemptive. To others it gives warrant to seek suffering, as if suffering was not what Jesus all his life tried to relieve. A third of the gospel tells of Jesus healing every kind of physical, mental, and emotional suffering he encountered. I think the cross is about the beauty and wonder of existence. To be called into a material world, to take a journey in time and space with God as my companion, to exist merely and wondrously in the miracle of sharing God's very existence, that is the meaning of the cross. Our existence, taken from nothingness, cannot be in the world without suffering, however small or great, infrequent or frequent. To live is to suffer, and to live, to be, to exist in even dire circumstance has a value beyond nothingness that can never be compared to anything at all. If there is a God, the creation will be fulfilled in God's eternal life, for God and goodness is convertible. The world will have a happy ending. In the meantime, creation and redemption suffer a time of the cross, which is why we can never lose sight of the cross. We live in a world where there is no escaping the passages and ravages of time and human decision. The choice we do have is to carry our cross hopefully or to drag it reluctantly. When we fall under its weight, we can only hope in God to lift us to do what can be done to relieve human suffering. Jesus did not explain the cross. Jesus carried his cross in solidarity with us, and his promise is that someday we will see that human existence was a blessing beyond all suffering, because the God of such mystery went before us.

Let us suppose Jesus died a natural death after many years in a quiet and hidden life in Nazareth. God's Son became human that we human beings might become divine. That embodiment of God is what saves us; that

acceptance of human vulnerability, mortality, and ineluctable death is what saves us. That Jesus must die
painfully is more an accident of history, the kind of fate
that most prophets of an inconvenient truth tend to endure, if they will not be silent in a politicized world. God
the Father did not require pain and suffering on the
cross as the price — a pound of flesh for humanity's sins.
The human conception and the human death of Jesus is
our salvation, even though the Calvary cross is a magnificent demonstration of how thoroughly human God
in Jesus became and how lavishly Jesus must have loved
us so to risk the cross. Jesus meekly accepts the price of
living the gospel he preached and walking the walk, not
just talking the talk.

A friend of mine cares for a dog who talks with sighs
and groans. It's so hard to be a dog. No doubt about it -
- ever alert, eager to please, ready to work, determined
to chase, busy all the time being the dog God made her
to be. At night this gentle German shepherd collaps-
es with what looks like exhaustion to me. It's so hard to
be a dog. And it's hard to be a human being. One need
not seek suffering or imagine that carrying the cross requires torment by evil perpetrators. Suffice each day's
burden. Every human being carries in their life's burden a cross just on the edge of their strength. Poor people suffer hunger; rich people suffer distress of another
kind as well. Students sweat exams and future employment; faculty sweat publication, tenure, promotion, and
retirement. Sooner or later the burden of suffering --
whether material, emotional, social, or spiritual makes

little difference -- weighs us down. The cross is with us always. We have to fly our plane to the ground; to attempt to glide into a landing is to fall. Being human can be so hard, and each person carries a cross in the form of some burden just beyond his or her strength now and here. Those who carry the cross display a peace that is earned. Those who drag their cross may be unwilling or they may be simply overwhelmed. In the end, the cross is how we say that to be human each and every day is not easy.

Everyone carries a burden just beyond their strength. Such is the omnipresent mystery of the cross in human life. The cross remains an equal opportunity lender. Everyone is in debt, rich or poor, well or sick, sooner or later. It is debt that weighs everyone down. No one finds heaven on earth. Appearances are deceptive. Suffering comes in all sizes and colors. We see the externals of a life of seeming happiness; we do not always know the miseries. We are present in their day; we are absent in their night. I grant there are lives that seem to have fallen into a hell on earth. There are unimaginable and unspeakable miseries almost everywhere. If I fall silent, it is because I do not know what to say. Job with his questions haunts human history. God never answered Job. He told him only that he was over his head and to shut up. Thereafter God speaks no other time in the Bible until God speaks his own Word, his beloved Son, Jesus the Christ, one of us, who dies on a cross so awful that we can never again doubt God suffers with us.

The outdoor stations at Notre Dame wind around

the southwest shoreline of St. Joseph's lake. A small path leads up through woods of very old oaks and sycamores looming overhead to a rise where a Calvary scene stands in life-size depiction – Jesus nailed to the cross with John and Mary on either side. Walk around the cross and from behind the figure of Jesus disappears. We rarely try to go behind the cross. We rarely ponder what is behind the cross. It is not the battered body of Jesus. What is behind the cross is the mystery of God's love for us. It is the mystery of suffering-love in a world we imagine could have been better without suffering. When we go to what is behind the cross we try to see the mind and heart of God. We discover behind the cross a God of love and a God of mystery -- not one or the other, but both.

CHAPTER FOUR
PRAYERS

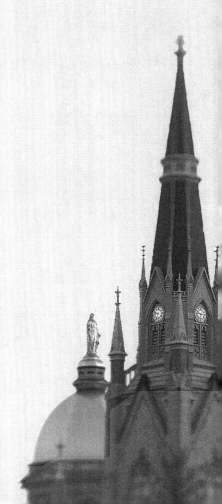

Confession

It should not be hard to find forgiveness at the University of Notre Dame. By and large the campus community would strive to live the Lord's Prayer in its "forgive us our trespasses as we forgive those who trespass against us." Living close to each other on a campus and in a residence hall will make for crossing all kinds of boundaries. "No Trespassing" signs do not work on a college campus, and most everyone knows their life belongs in part to others as well as themselves. Whether borrowing or imposing, presuming or leaving destructive footprints, life together will test our willingness to forgive others as we hope to be forgiven in turn. Friends all engage in the kind of listening that is forgiveness. In the end, however, forgiveness is about our changing from a closed heart to an open one, from a hateful heart to a loving heart, from hard-hearted to soft-hearted. We must change to be forgiven, and we know we are forgiven when we have changed. Conversation with those who are willing to listen to us remains the lubricant of such change. God's grace and our determination do the rest.

GOD IS THE TRUE MASTER of all kinds of forgiveness. God forgives us all the time, even without our asking, because God is love, and such love "bears all things, believes all things, hopes all things, endures all things. Love never fails" (1 Cor 13: 7-8). Parents forgive the sins of their children, even as they ask for apology and repentance and firm purpose of amendment. They may ask for confession, but not for their sake in order to be placated from hurt and anger. Loving parents ask for confession for the sake of the child they love. And so with God. Confession is good for us, not good for God, who needs nothing and has no anger toward us. We need to confess God's mercy, God knows.

Not only is God always forgiving us and always ready to hear our plea for forgiveness, for we need to express our sorrow, but other people forgive our sins readily. Even the bartender who listens to a tale of woe offers forgiveness in a very sympathetic listening. Families forgive one another even when a word is not spoken, but the next meal is taken together. One can speak with the eloquent silence of one's demeanor as well as with words, even if words may be best. Friends and confidants forgive. Forgiveness, just as love, is common as the grass beneath our feet.

So, one might ask, why sacramental confession? Why ask forgiveness of the Church in the person of a priest, whom you do not even know. For starters, if you talk with a priest rather than with a friend, you may receive a less varnished acceptance with a challenge to avoid the denial to which we are all prone. Friends do not want to weaken friendship, and they may choose their words to that end. Friends are not necessarily spiritually minded or theologically savvy, and even well-intentioned advice may be less helpful than the wise counsel of an experienced priest. But, most of all, the priest speaks words one can imagine as God's words of forgiveness, embodied however imperfectly in the priest's concern. We hear a word from God in whatever the priests says, and the words of absolution are the Church's validation of the love of God for all us sinners. How beautiful those words: "God the Father of mercies, through the death and resurrection of His Son, has reconciled the world to himself and sent the Holy Spirit among us for the forgiveness of sins. Through the ministry of the Church, may God give you pardon and peace, and I absolve you from your sins, in the name of the Father, the Son, and the Holy Spirit."

Moreover, the priest is the official ordained delegate of the whole people of God, the community that is the Church, in order to represent them all. We cannot possible ask in person forgiveness of everyone we have harmed, and our sins diminish to a degree everyone, because we are in this life together. Both the good and the bad that we do inevitably impact everyone else. To ask of the priest who represents everyone is to ask forgiveness of everyone, and to hear the Church's words of absolution spoken by the priest is to receive a consoling forgiveness from everyone – from God first of all and most of all, who changes our heart in forgiving us, but also from the people of God, who allow their priests to speak for them.

The Woman Taken in Adultery

Young men and young women together for four years in a relatively small campus presents a tension both troublesome and delightful. Raging hormones may be an exaggeration, but bodily sexual maturity is not. In earlier times marriage and children would have been well on the way by the time of college years. My experience as a priest tells me that nobody's sexual life is altogether tidy. We may wish it were so, but it is not. We may even employ a double standard to tidy up male behavior. We may persecute gays in order to find someone else to blame. The "Sluttle" title was tagged by some to the "Shuttle" bus that runs between St. Mary's College and Notre Dame. Shame and humiliation are part of an old game that the best defense is a good offense. Internet pornography cruises this campus and every campus. The "Vagina Monologues" have been controversial on this campus and others Catholic campuses. In matters sexual we are not comfortable, and spin of every kind is concocted when we are reluctant to proclaim that no one is without sin.

THE STORY OF JESUS and the woman taken in adultery may be the most empathetic snapshot of Jesus in his compassion to be found in all the gospels (See Jn 8: 1-11). Perhaps a late addition to John's gospel, or a misplaced section of Luke's gospel, it is evident the Christian community in its early days insisted this story must be told. Jesus defends a woman whose guilt is never in question, though attenuating circumstances might have been ignored. Jesus defends a woman that men want to kill, thinking, perhaps conveniently, that they are doing God's will and keeping the Law, though no man involved in the adultery itself is brought forward. She is alone, and Jesus is this woman's only friend.

This gospel story touches us all. No one, man or woman, enjoys a sexual life that is without sin. The instinctual forces of sexual attraction and desire have made monkeys of us all one time or another. No one's videotaped sexual life would not bring embarrassment and some degree of shame and guilt. We are not masters of our own house. We often find ourselves on a runaway horse bent on the need to be loved, to continue life, and to satisfy a nagging insistence for what we hardly know what.

They drag her in front of Jesus from her bed of sinfulness, and one suspects all undressed for public inspection. Righteous, they want to pulverize her body with stones thrown in anger and righteousness. They are us at times. They also want Jesus to approve their upholding of the Law, and God's Law, they say. Jesus stoops down and draws on the earth with his finger. Is this an enactment of God writing commandments on stone for Moses, which commandments Israel never kept well – neither the men nor the women? Does Jesus writes something of the sins of the men who hold stones in their hands? I do not know, but I rather think Jesus was doodling in the sand out of embarrassment at the predicament of this woman whose eyes he could hardly bear to meet. "Let the one who is without sin cast the first stone," and they all go away, beginning with the eldest, and that, we can assume, tells us that ours sins accumulate with the years. None of us are innocent. "Has no one condemned you?" says Jesus to the woman. "No one, Lord," she says to him. "Neither do I," Jesus says, and now the reader with any heart must weep, knowing divine compassion revealed so tenderly. "But, go and sin no more," Jesus says. Sin will only make her more unhappy, more embarrassed, and will not solve whatever the sadness, or injustice, or willfulness in her life, which brought her to that bed and then to near death. We can never snatch our own happiness, and two wrongs never make a right. But God knows, and Jesus feels that this woman deserves compassion more than blame. May we all be so blessed.

Mercy and Forgiveness

Mercy is yet more than forgiveness. Mercy is a free lunch, a piece of pure good fortune, an unearned grace. Most students along the way recognize that someone in their schooling gave them a break they did not deserve, either because they were so young or because the giver of mercy was so good to them. Grandparents often embody mercy. Many of us have known "angels" in our life, who appeared without due cause and gave us counsel or opportunity that we in retrospect recognize made all the difference in our future life. Many of our Notre Dame students come from broken families. For better or for worse they have had to deal with forgiveness. All of us, students and non-students, come from dysfunctional families at some times and in some ways. We always hurt the ones we love. Deeply understanding forgiveness is one of life's mercies.

A MORE POIGNANT STORY in the gospels may not be found than the story of the unnamed woman who washes the feet of Jesus with her tears of sorrow and then lets down her long hair to dry them (See Lk 7: 41-50). The listener of this story has a crucial curve to negotiate. Some

115

translations in English round the corner and others go off the road and miss the depth of this love story. Much is forgiven her because she loved much is not the moral of the story. That understanding may be true in human affairs, where human forgiveness must be earned by repentance and willing recompense. Not so with the forgiveness of God in the forgiveness that Jesus embodies when he tells a more profound truth. She must have been forgiven much; hence she is loving so much. In short, she has first been loved well, and thus she loves in return. It is never the other way round. By our initiative in loving we do not win God's forgiveness and love. The initiative is always from God. We have nothing without God's grace. The point of this Lucan gospel story is precisely that she does not earn forgiveness by her generosity. God's prior generosity, God's prior love for her, God's prior forgiveness gratuitously given enables her to respond with a love given now to Jesus in response to the love God gave her all undeserved. We know hurt people hurt people. We also know that loved people love people. We must first be loved by God, by parents, by others in order to love ourselves and then to reach out to others. No one loves who has not somehow somewhere been loved before. One has first to receive, then to give. One has first to catch the ball before throwing it. One has first to know love in the form of forgiveness for what one has done or for who one is. Only then can one wash feet with tears of repentance and thanksgiving, and take down one's hair without shame or thought of sinning in order to dry the washed feet with one's own body. Only those who know how much they have been loved can do so. "Felix culpa," which means happy fault, is a theological understanding that given the love of God's forgiveness human beings may be better off with God than we would have been without our unspoken plea for mercy.

Forgiveness that is so generously given as love is given should enable us to overcome our regrets. We will always have remorse when we hurt the ones we love, or would have loved had we known better. But such sorrow for our sins is not regret for our living our life for better or for worse. Regrets are the lingering suspicion that forgiveness and gratuitous love -- given our guilt -- are simply too good to be true. In truth, however, God is infinitely better at mercy than we can comprehend.

Conversion and the Father Of Mercies

God's mercy comes to us in the moment of the conversion of our hearts. Falling in love is a secular conversion story, and on the campus of any college one can attest to a changed outlook and behavior when a love-relationship is blossoming in the life of a college student. Resentment and indifference are replaced with gratitude and solicitude for the beloved and all of the life around him or her that is so enhanced. Roommates in the residence halls at Notre Dame are randomly chosen, and one of the conversions of college years is the overcoming of prejudice about someone of a different race or religion who is encountered, then understood, and then loved as the roommate that one was given but now has chosen. The "Urban Plunge" at Notre Dame introduces students of privilege to an underworld of poverty that they may have read about but never seen up close, touched upon, or much thought about. To understand is to love. Most people are doing the best they know how. Conversion of our hearts and our judgments remains one of the most cherished outcomes of an integral college education.

THE PARABLE OF THE PRODIGAL SON is best understood as the story of the prodigal father, whose love expressed as forgiveness knows no limits. Hungry and abused after squandering the inheritance he prematurely demanded of his father, the younger son returns home with no other hope than gaining employment. He assumes he can never be restored to his father as the son he once was. He only expects that maybe his father's pity will land him a job as an employee with food enough to live. He does not tell his father he is sorry. He only says that "he has sinned and deserves no longer to be called his son" (Lk 15: 21). His father will hear none of this, and immediately embraces him, puts the shoes of the rich on his feet, and the ring of the distinguished on his finger, and insists that the fatted calf be prepared for a home-coming grand party. "For this my son was lost and he has been found. I thought he was dead, and lo he is alive." (Lk 15:32). Both sons misunderstood their father. The elder son thought he had earned his father's love by his good behavior, and hence he resents the party for his sinful brother. The younger son thought he irrevocably lost his father's love by his bad behavior, and hence he expected no reprieve. Both sons are dead wrong. They are loved by their father because they are his sons. Nothing the two sons can do, for good or for bad, can change the love that God the Father gives for his children, and perhaps the more so the more miserable their condition when they return home for mercy's sake. Bad behavior is not applauded, of course, but not because it hurts the father, but because it hurts the child the father loves and others as well.

How to Pray

There are some fifty chapels on the Notre Dame Campus. Every residence hall has its chapel, most of them very beautiful and contemplative sacred spaces in buildings that otherwise rock with youthful enthusiasms. Public prayer through liturgical prayer is hardly lacking. There is a mass celebrated for happy events and for sad events. Even athletics at Notre Dame have a prayer dimension, small as it may be in the context of an active sport. Classroom prayers raise no eyebrows, and grace before meals can be done in public without embarrassment. Prayer is part of the life of the Notre Dame campus.

THE DISCIPLES ASKED JESUS to teach them how to pray. If you want to pray, follow the example of those first disciples of Jesus. To pray, Jesus said to them, begin with but one word. In praying, "Father," you may well have said it all. Prayer is always a recognition – who we are and who God is. Each of us is a child of God, created by God, loved by our Father in heaven, who made us out of nothing but pure love for us. We may not now at this moment of prayer feel much loved, and we may have mixed feelings in our memory of our human father. None of that

120

matters to the heart of prayer, which is to trust God to be beyond what we even dare imagine.

The Lord's Prayer is a distillation of whatever prayer-instruction in word and in example that Jesus left his disciples. Divided into two parts, and with somewhat different wording in Matthew and in Luke, the Lord's Prayer begins with calling on the Father, whose only beloved Son became our brother. As God with us, he died in the torture of this world, both with us and most of all for us.

"Hallowed be thy name" invites us to stop and think. Our life is distracted. We do not pray frequently. We still do not know how to pray well. We hardly want to pray. We know we should pray. It's a mess all too often. But, take heart. Prayer is a recognition that God is beyond us. God is awesome. God is holy, and what God is doing in the world and in us remains more important and more lasting that anything we are doing. We forget that God can do anything and everything. We forget God is doing anything and everything. Prayer is simple recognition that we are not orphans. We are invited to hold the hand of the man. We are invited to trust that our life is truly in God's hands. Hard to believe and almost too good to be true. Trust God. Relax in God. Let go; let God. If God is your copilot, swap seats. Prayer is that recognition that God is God, whose providence touches all our lives, past, present and future, and covers them all always and all ways with God's sovereign love. We need to let God be God and stop ourselves from trying to play out a miserable imitation of God.

"Thy Kingdom Come" and "Thy will be done" but echo the hallowed name of the Father, who, in giving us His beloved Son gave us everything. We pray that God's will be done, but not in asking for a sentence from above to be imposed upon us. God wants nothing more from us than what we want in the depths of our soul made in the image of God. What we truly want deep down, God wants, but not what mimetic desire, fostered by our advertising culture, would sell us as the good life. Giving our life in love and service remains the good life, and that self-sacrificing love is buried deep in every human heart. God's will emerges into God's Kingdom when that love deeply buried in us become our way of life day by day. In sum, how should we pray? As the Lord prayed, I want to say, and in recognition of the Father's love, and in the laying down of our life for others as Jesus did in love for us and for the Father, whose great love for us Jesus embodied.

Why Pray

If we are people of prayer, we all promise at times to pray for someone else in trouble. We pray for ourselves in trouble as well. Count the candles in the Grotto at Notre Dame, and you will understand that prayer for human needs is alive and well on campus. There would be even more candles lit, if the Fire Department could allow yet more heat in such a confined space, even though an outdoor space. What else can we do may well be a reason to pray. We are so often helpless to protect and cherish those we love. Problems on our small campus and problems in our large world overwhelm all our efforts. We are not masters in our own house. That fragility and vulnerability of the human condition is surely one of the things that college students learn, should they have not learned that wisdom before they arrived on campus. Perhaps one may drift unaware through high school. The need for prayer comes clearer with the human maturity achieved in college years, and most of the men and women whom good parents entrust to Notre Dame are changed for the better in these final years of their formal education.

IF GOD KNOWS WHAT we need before we ask, why pray? God does not need to be informed by us. God does not need our pleading to lavish his love upon us. God cares for us more than we can possibly care for ourselves. And yet we need to pray, if for no other reason than we have a body with emotions that must speak and a heart that hopes to be heard. As children we did not need to beg our breakfast, but we needed to learn to say "please." We wanted to say "thank you" when we were mindful of how hungry we were and how helpless to provide for ourselves in our vulnerability at that age. Prayer is always the emotional expression of need and an overall cry of the heart for what we need to take care of us. We pray at day's end for only one thing, that God take care of us — and indeed all of us.

In the Gospels, Jesus prayed, and that alone is a good reason for why we also should pray. Jesus prayed in the Garden of Gethsemani. He asked to live. Jesus did not want to die. He pleaded with his Father for his life. He prayed, as we do, that God might take care of him in his hour of dire need. And God heard his prayer. His Father did cherish the life of his Son. But note, God the Father did not answer Jesus' prayer in the way Jesus proposed. Man proposes; God disposes. In the end God took care of Jesus' life more profoundly and more thoroughly than Jesus even dreamed.

Whatever the outcome of our prayer, whatever way God disposes to take care of us, our prayer changes us. God does not need to change, as if God were ignorant or indifferent and could be roused by our prayers if only frequent and loud enough. It is we who need to change. We need to reorder our priorities. We ourselves need to claim more profound values. We need new eyes to see God's beneficence. We ourselves need to answer many prayers, instead of expecting God to do what human beings are able to do if willing to meet the human needs of others. We need to let others help us, and we need to help them. We need to believe in our prayer as a window into God's providential love, even if God's ways are not our ways. All prayers are answered by God, and indeed are being answered even before we ask. Yet, we need to ask, to say "please" and "thank you," to see with God's eyes how "to those who love God all things commingle unto good." Prayer draws us into the mystery of God. Prayer teaches us patience, humility, and most of all trust. God who created us out of nothing will take care to fulfill our lives out of everything about which we pray. Prayer is our living belief in that boundless providence of God.

Can We Pray Always?

Late adolescence and young adulthood are the times when most men and women fall in love. If that sounds too romantic for this generation, whose music seems so realistic and even strident, there is still a truth about college years. We are likely to be awed. Education may implicate a recognition of the beauty of art and literature, the integrity of truth and its wonders, the goodness of self-sacrifice and serving others. We may even come to know God, and falling in love with God can be real and not just romantic. Students at Notre Dame do seek spiritual direction. They want to know how to pray. They may feel they have been deprived of their heritage by the religious-culture wars. They do not have the foundational teaching that some earlier generations, drilled in Thomistic philosophy and theology, may take for granted. Can we pray always will not seem a strange question to college students in search for someone transcendent to whom they might belong.

THREE TIMES A DAY most of us find time to eat and drink. A blessing before meals or a thanksgiving at the end of meals remains an ancient tradition that encourages praying always. We do not forget to eat. We would not forget to pray at least three times a day, if we always attached a prayer to our daily bread. Not only should we attend our food and drink for its taste, quality, and appearance, relishing what we have been given and what human artifice has made of the bounty of the earth, but also in our prayers at mealtime we might cultivate our awareness of our utter dependency on God's world and on others within it for our sustenance. We are not self-sufficient. We do not make food within ourselves, and "what have you that you have not received"? (1 Cor 4:7) When someone feeds us, and someone always is feeding us, whether recognized by us or not, they give us our very body and our very next breath.

To that next breath let us turn in our attempt to find a way to pray always and to attend to what God is doing in our lives. Twelve times a minute we breathe in and we breathe out. We can live but four minutes without breathing, and in any bodily accident the most important first-aid is to ensure breathing. Air is our life. The word for spirit in Hebrew is the word for breath. And when we breathe forth our spirit, we die. Our last breath is our "last breath." The precariousness of our very existence is well monitored in our breathing. Many of the contemplatives and mystics of the world claim that attentiveness to one's breathing is a road into deep prayer. We take in the world with each breath; we warm what we have been given with our blood, and we return what we have received to the world around us. Breathing is the master metaphor of exchange that is at the heart of all human intercourse. We receive love and we give love. We are given our existence by God with each inhalation, and we return to God our existence with each exhalation. How often during the day might we attend to the mystery of our creation from nothing by the love of God for us? As often as we breathe I want to say. Frequently I am vaguely aware of my breathing, and especially when I pause to collect my wits or attend to God more explicitly. I can breathe in the blessings of God and breathe back thanks and praise for what God is always and everywhere doing. Breathing in is reminiscent of grace before meals and the life-reception of morning prayer. Breathing out is reminiscent of thanksgiving after meals and the life-surrendering of evening prayer. "I live, now not I, but Christ lives in me" (Gal 2:20) writes St. Paul. We are temples of the Holy Spirit (1 Cor 6:19). The breath of God that awakened Adam's clay continues to infuse our every breath. We are suffused in God, who is more part of us than we are part of ourselves, and yet we are alive and breathing on our own. To be attentive to what is the reality of our self and our lives is to be aware of God. To pay attention to what God is ever doing is to pray and to pray always. Poets pay attention to metaphors; detectives pay attention to clues; artists pay attention to colors and shapes; novelists pay attention to stories; prayerful people pay attention to God's pro-viding on their behalf. We sleep, we eat, we breathe. Perhaps we can pray always.

Can Prayer Change Anything?

In so many situations in daily life, on campus or at home, we can only say "I will pray for you." We are frequently asked to keep others in our prayers. Nothing could be more taken for granted at Notre Dame than this. Prayer is not a waste of time. But, the question remains. Does prayer change anything? There can be little doubt that when we pray we want to change something. Our prayer is rarely a simple one of "Thy will be done." That routine prayer tends to be the resignation of someone who had proposed very detailed answers to prayer and has come to recognize that sometimes God says "no." Pleading with God does us no good and seems to make God look hard-to-please. We do not plead for what is truly good from someone who truly loves us. It is polite to ask, but it is not necessary to beg. But, in our prayer so often we want to change something. We want to make someone well who is sick, to make peace instead of war, to find happiness instead of misery. Surely God's ways are not our ways. Perhaps we do not profoundly understand the mystery of the cross. And yet, we pray for God to intervene on our behalf. Does prayer, however, really change anything?

When we pray for this or for that, does prayer change anything? Will the outcome be in any way different had we not prayed? Let us first of all ask a prior question. When we pray for this or for that, does prayer change anyone? Short answer: (1) Prayer does not change God, who already knows all that we need and who because of God's everlasting and unconditional love for us needs no pleading on our part to give us all that we need. (2) Prayer does change us. We become more aware of what values matter in life, of how God's ways are not our ways, and of the many ways God providentially answers our prayers besides the short-sighted ways we propose to God. (3) All those who hear our prayers or hear of our prayers are changed, because challenged to answer them in the human ways open to them.

To come back to the main question — does prayer change anything? Short answer: sometimes there are delayed cures for this or for that (even aspirin takes time to heal a headache); rarely there are "miracles," because miracles suggest the strategy of a God who must adjust the future as that God learns from our free behaviors what the future will hold. In truth, God does not learn the future from us, or see the future from some higher vantage point. God does not learn the future; God creates the future, and thus God does not need to mend the future with miracles, other than the daily miracles of blades of grass and the wonders of the human heart and spirit, and so much more.

So, tell me, why should we pray if God is creating the future, and with our true and real freedom included?

Short answer: so that we might contribute freely and knowingly a piece of the future. How so? God created the whole world "in the beginning" from nothing. Logically that is impossible, but logically impossible is possible to God. "In the ending" of the world, God will have created a new heaven and a new earth from everything. By everything, I mean everything. Even sin serves. God writes straight with crooked lines. "For those who love God, all things commingle unto good." Not a drop was wasted. No tear was shed in vain. In sum, we pray so that our lives play a part in the "everything" that God is taking even now to create a new heaven and new earth from everything "in the ending." May our lives be deliberately, willingly, and lovingly contributed to God as an offering. We say to God: this predicament is my piece of the puzzle; this is my prayer; this is my heart's concern. Dear God, please use everything about me revealed in my prayers and in my living as part of the new creation, the new heaven and earth that you are creating out of everything. Creation from nothing is a marvel; creation from everything is a marvel squared. Our prayers are always answered. Nothing of our joy or sorrow will be wasted. The only question is whether we trust God to create the future, or whether we cling to planning the future according to our lights and our desires, futile as they prove to be. "Thy will be done" is never a prayer of resignation, but one always with its moment of grace and truth.

Morning Prayer

Who taught us as children to say our morning prayers? Where did our faith enjoy its birth? Morning sunrise is a birthing of the world, as sunset seems the dying of the light. Those alums of Notre Dame old enough to remember lights out at 11PM in the residence halls, know more of the morning light. Various in-hall misdemeanors earned one a trip to the University Gate-shack where one was obliged to sign in at 6AM. "Dawn Patrol" was what students affectionately named it. In point of fact, dawn is long before sunrise, and not everyone has seen a dawn in the very early hours of the morning, when the first light comes into the black night sky and the birds of summer begin to sing. It is a unique time to praise God, who has gifted us with existence.

MORNING PRAYER is a simple praise of God. Did this beautiful world not exist and did we not exist, there would nothing to be said and no one to say it. As things now exist and we among them all, there is so much to say. Most of all, we recognize we will never say enough. God's wonder-world overwhelms us. We may well find morning a time for the prayer of silence and awe. What

God is and what God is doing exceeds everything we can comprehend. If God were not for us, nothing we could do could convert the Almighty. If God is for us, and Jesus is our pledge of our hope in God, then there is nothing we can do to escape God. We do not win God; we do not lose God. The initiative is all God's, and the essence of prayer is praise and worship that the infinite God has taken us to heart. Morning Prayer remains essentially worship and awe and wonder. God loves us. God has given us his only and beloved Son, and in giving us Jesus, God has given us everything.

Congruent with the prayer of morning praise of God is our awareness of how much we need to change. Forgiveness from God is not about God changing from angry with us to pleased with us. Forgiveness is the gift of God that changes our heart. In forgiveness we receive an ever-growing change of heart that stems directly from God's great love for us human beings. We know we need a change of heart. We are so often cold-hearted and hard-hearted. Morning Prayer is coming alive from the night of sleep and coming alive from the darkness of a self-centered heart. In Morning Prayer we are a child of the universe and a child of God. Our awareness of God's goodness stems from what the light all around us reveals and from the inner light that shows us we can be changed. As the world was created from nothing, God can and will create a clean heart in us from our less-than-nothing – our sinfulness that can talk back to God and pretend to give God grief. As the light of morning is born from the dark of night, as we were born into this world from our mother's womb, so we await our birth into eternal life when morning will be forever.

Evening Prayer

Alums of a certain age will remember "night check" at Notre Dame. In the residence halls the lights were disconnected at bedtime, and just prior to that moment of darkness, the assistant rector on each floor took bed check, or "night check." You had to be in your room or you were absence-without-leave. There were ways around it all, including creative wiring, but it was not all bad. The priests and staff of the residence hall came to have some conversation with almost everyone night after night. Day and night were separated as day and night in the Genesis creation story. It was a kind of night prayer, and those students who turned in when the lights went out no doubt said their version of night prayer. Monks sing their Compline. The Basilica at Notre Dame celebrates its Sunday Evening Vespers with music and prayer. Most of us have plenty to be thankful for and much to be sorrowful for. Most of all we thank God at night that we are alive, and that our heart both beats and cares about how we are living our life with God as our hope and our help.

NIGHT PRAYER brings back memories of childhood. "Do not forget to say your prayers before you go to bed." One's first sacramental confession readily included "I forgot my evening prayers (xx many times)." Night prayer rightly was thought important because sleep is a rehearsal of death, and death our birth into eternal life. Unconscious sleep, just as loss of memory when we are awake, reminds us of our mortality. Some day, some night, we will awaken in the Kingdom of God and life everlasting. And so we pray in the silence and in the dark.

"If you build it, they will come" was the claim of the popular baseball movie, "Field of Dreams." The stars of yesteryear returned to a sandlot park built in their honor and with belief in their lasting fame. They came from out of the cornfield to the diamond in the middle of nowhere. Awake in my bed, I too call on the Communion of Saints. If you pray, they will come. And they do. I call in my parents and grandparents, my dear friends and mentors, those who died in wars and those who were tortured to death. I call in the executed criminals and my favorite saints of long ago. My heart expands for everyone who ever lived and died, and I peek for a moment at the heart of Jesus who said: "No one that the Father has given me have I lost" (Jn 17:12). "Our Father" is the Father of us all, no matter when or where we have lived, no matter our death be easy or hard, no matter our moral life be seen from the outside as good or bad. If you pray to them, they will come. I ask Dismas, the good thief of the cross, to remember me as Jesus remembered him. I tell Pilate's wife that I remember her, and I want Princess Diana on my side of the bed and Mother Teresa on the other. I find in the night that it is easy to love every one of God's own children. If you call on them in the night in prayer, they will come. Night prayer as one grows older expands into hours of quiet and prayerful sleeplessness.

On a vacation trip to the north woods of Wisconsin I had made a reservation at a motel near Land O' Lakes, where Notre Dame preserves a large tract of unspoiled wilderness with some twenty plus lakes available for high-level research and some low-level angling. The motel was closed, because the son of the woman who ran the business had just graduated from high school and then took his life. I stopped, but I had no occasion to meet her, because the funeral was held that day. On my return to Notre Dame I passed the motel, whose roadsign in capital letters read: "Good night, Moon." I know the book. I know the story. I pray with that young boy now. I know there are many kinds of night prayer.

Eucharistic Prayer

Some people worry about the "Real Presence" in the minds of young college-age Catholics. Do they believe in the "Real Presence"? Dorm masses on a Sunday evening are well attended, but the whole liturgy may seem to some more a social event than a sacral event. The innovation of a bow before receiving Holy Communion was thought a help by the Vatican to remind the recipients of the "Real Presence," which they are not to take for granted and all too casually. Students might well not give a ready account of the theology of "Real Presence." They do not know much about medieval theology, and that is a pity. And yet, such theology is not the core of belief in the wonder of the Eucharist.

FOR A CHILD TO RECEIVE their first Holy Communion, they need not know anything of the theology of the Eucharist. They need only know that this bread is special, and that Jesus is really present. Transubstantiation is a wonderful theology of the Eucharist, but what we put our faith in is never the theology but rather the mystery of the Eucharist, which even a child can adore.

Which person would you say is really present to you?

Close your eyes. On one side of you is a stranger and on the other side your best friend. That friend tiptoes away unbeknown to you and is whisked away in a fast automobile many miles away. After many minutes you open your eyes. Which of the persons that stood beside you was really present? Was it the stranger inches from your shoulder but far from your heart, or the friend miles from your side but close to your heart? Who is really present? What is real presence?

Just as the friend present to our heart and the stranger present to our body, the real presence of the Eucharist suggests many real presences. Christ is always present in his people, in us, in the assembled congregation at the Eucharist. We are the body of Christ here and now. Christ is present in the priest who stands in his place and speaks words of mystery in Christ's name. Christ is present in the Holy Scriptures read to us, which conclude not with "this (reading) is the Word of the Lord, but simply the "Word of the Lord," who is the Word of God, who "in the beginning was the Word and the Word was with God, and the Word was God."

Were it possible, the whole Christian people would assemble in one church, where the bishop would preside over his flock and undertake the work of Christ. No doubt the city would be Rome, where the Basilica of St. Peter would encompass everyone. Were we further able to miniaturize ourselves, we would all fit on one altar. We are the bread and we are the wine. Because we cannot all fit on the altar, where we would stand at the foot of the Calvary cross, we substitute bread and wine that are our food and drink, shorthand for our life and its sustenance. Just as an animal was sacrificed in the Temple as a substitute for us, so we bring bread and wine in procession to the altar, because we cannot all fit upon the altar with our bodies. But note, although the bread and wine do change into the body of Christ, the more profound mystery is that we change. We are changed into the body of Christ. That is the mystery of the Eucharist. God changes bread for no other miracle than to change us. We are changed. We like to say we become the food we eat; we are the food we eat. But that is not exactly so. We do not become a tomato; the tomato becomes us. In the Eucharist, however, it is so. We become what we eat. We eat the body of Christ and we change. We become what we eat. We become the body of Christ. We are changed, converted, and transformed, and that conversion is a greater miracle than the creation of the world or the transubstantiation of the bread and wine. We change. That is the miracle of the Eucharist, and that is the Real Presence of Christ in the Church.

Hail Mary

Every evening at the Grotto of Notre Dame, for as far back as I can remember, the rosary has been recited at the Grotto. The group is small and undistinguished, but they believe in the rosary. How often this prayer to our Lady of Notre Dame is recited on campus may never be known. More than one thinks would be my estimate. The bells in the Basilica steeple sound the Angelus at noon, and carillon in the steeple slowly chimes the alma mater, "Notre Dame, our Mother," at 10 PM of an evening. The glimpse of the Dome of Notre Dame in sunlight or in moonlight can take your breath away. Its appearance to my eyes always brings a Hail Mary prayer to my lips.

CARYLL HOUSELANDER called Mary "the reed of God." Her book, so titled, is one of the very best ever written about the Blessed Mother. God's song sounded in the body of Mary and in her whole life. It was not her melody. She was the fluted reed of God's melody. The Hail Mary prayer repeats the words of the angel Gabriel and the words of Mary's cousin, Elizabeth. Not a word of Mary has been recorded, and the Gospel hymn we call the "Magnificat" seems well cribbed from the "Song of Hannah" sung long before Mary of Nazareth. She was the incomparable song-reed of God, nonetheless the humble handmaid of the Lord, the unique instrument of humankind's marriage to God. If the humble were to be exalted, Mary belongs on the top of the Golden Dome. She would not place herself above, but we cannot resist doing so in our devotion to the woman who brought our God into this world and shaped his life on earth.

Prayer to Mary as woman and mother "at the hour of our death" may trail roots that go deep into the archetypal unconscious of human beings. Women nurse their children at birth with the milk of their body, and they nurse them at death with the care of their hearts. Motherhood is a perduring lifelong relationship in most people's experience. Women await the birthing; and they wait beside the death-bed of the dying and arrange the funeral rituals. The newborn child is immediately placed in the arms of the happy mother to behold in joy, and the dead body of her child is placed on the lap of the unhappy mother to mourn in sorrow. Madonna and Pieta. Mary as joyful mother with child in the Madonna has been depicted no more poignantly than Mary as sorrowful mother in the Pieta. Mother of the living and mother of the dead. Life-accepting in the beginning and life-accepting in the ending. The sovereignty of God is never more manifest than at birth, which seems so improbable, and resurrection from death that seems so impossible. Womankind has long been connected with the mystery of life and of death coming from the hands of God. Only Mary knew Jesus from the womb to the tomb, from birth into this life to birth into eternal life, that is, the resurrection of the body and life everlasting. No wonder Christians love to pray: "Hail Mary, full of grace, the Lord is with you."

CHAPTER FIVE
SCRIPTURES

Saint Joseph

A large statue of Saint Joseph stands just east of Old College, the very first and still standing building of Notre Dame. Joseph holds a young-boy Jesus in his arms and he presents a strong masculine image. The Brothers of Holy Cross, whose patron saint is Saint Joseph, came as a small band with Father Sorin to where the Log Chapel and Old College can be seen to this day. Father Sorin's mind and heart built Notre Dame, but the hands and backs of the brothers carried the brick and mortar and hewed the logs. Saint Joseph is the patron of workers. He was a carpenter and more like today's construction worker who builds houses. In the Basilica of the Sacred Heart a whole wall fresco on the east side of the sanctuary portrays Joseph dying in his bed, with Jesus on one side of him and Mary on the other. No wonder the Church holds him the patron of the dying. Joseph lives on at Notre Dame in the many blue-collar workers, and the staff of men and women who run the university in so many quotidian matters. He was the foster father of Jesus and protector of Mary, and Saint Joseph, we pray, watches over Our Lady, Notre Dame, even to this day.

IMAGINE JOSEPH at breakfast in Nazareth -- the Immaculate Conception on one side of the table and the Incarnation of God on the other side of the table. I smile whenever I think of Joseph. He had to have a sense of humor. Joseph does not appear again in the Gospels after the visit to Jerusalem in Luke's account, when the adolescent Jesus teaches the doctors of the Law in the Temple. Mary and Joseph search for him in the caravan walking home to Nazareth after the Festival, and they return to Jerusalem to find him. Jesus insists he must be about his Father's business. We never hear of Joseph again. He is not mentioned in the Passion narratives in which many minor characters play a role. Mary appears at the foot of the cross and even amid the apostles when the Holy Spirit descends among them at Pentecost. It has been assumed that Joseph died before Jesus began his public ministry, and that likely he was older than Mary, perhaps a widower, well suited to be her husband and guardian and foster father of Jesus.

I want to argue for one unique virtue in Joseph among the many attributed to him. Granted he provided for the Holy Family. He taught Jesus to be "the carpenter's son," and very likely Jesus in his hidden life in Nazareth for most of his life worked as a craftsman and builder. What Joseph did that is unique and for which he should be held in highest esteem is this. Joseph gave Jesus the human meaning of the word "father" by his example as a father to Jesus, and that has made all the difference. One assumes that Jesus had to be taught to walk and to talk. He learned the meaning of "father" from Joseph.

Jesus spoke of his Father in heaven, "Our Father who art in heaven." One can consider the Lord's Prayer as a distillation of the entire gospel, and one can consider the one word, "Abba, Father," as the distillation of the Lord's Prayer. "Who sees me sees the Father," Jesus tells Phillip (Jn 12: 45). What Jesus reveals throughout all his life and in all his words and deeds is the face of his Father. We will never fathom God who is infinite mystery. We have come to know through Jesus that God the Father is not aloof or removed in his love for this world. "God the Father" and "Joseph the father" remain in harmony, even if the one is beyond the other, as the divine is beyond the human, In Jesus, however, God's divinity and our humanity do embrace forever.

John the Baptist

College years reap the efforts of much parenting and mentoring. With Junior Parents' Weekend at Notre Dame, the students have their chance to thank their parents, and I hope implicitly to thank all those in our students' lives in loco parentis. *Rectors and teachers come easily to mind, and they are included in some ways in this weekend celebration. "What have you that you have not received" (1 Cor 4:7) is as true today as it was when Saint Paul wrote it. Teachers and students alike at any university stand on the shoulders of others. If we see further, we owe others who prepared the way. Elders, heroes, saints, prophets -- we know much about passing on the baton in the race to the true, the good, and the beautiful. One of our tasks in our later years is to encourage our replacement and to bless those who are young and who may well in the long run be wiser than we were. John the Baptist was the forerunner for the blessed one who changed everything in the world forever.*

TODAY IS THE FEAST of the beheading of John the Baptist. Strange that we call it a feast day, but no doubt we wish to celebrate the life and honor the martyr's death of this great prophet, who gave his life for the telling of the truth to a king who did not want to hear it. Jesus said of John: "No one greater that John the Baptist is born of woman" (Lk7:28). John said of Jesus: "I must decrease and he must increase" (Jn 3:30). John's birth is celebrated on June 25th. The sun in the northern hemisphere then begins to decrease and reaches its lowest point in late December at Christmas time. Jesus is born on December 25th, just when the light of the sun begins to increase and bring back life to this winter earth.

"I am not worthy to tie his sandals" (Lk 3:16) John says of Jesus, who comes in humility to John for baptism. We put dirty clothes in clean water to wash them clean. Jesus was innocent, and when he stepped into the waters of the Jordan, he made those waters clean. John, however, did mentor Jesus. He taught him how to preach and set him upon a vocation to baptize. Someone had to educate Jesus in the ways of a prophet, as someone had to teach him to walk, to talk, and to tie his sandals. John was his teacher, whom Jesus would soon surpass. John could only wash the surface with his baptism, and his converts reverted all too easily and quickly to their previous lives. Jesus discovered that he could baptize with water and the Spirit. Jesus changed hearts from within where water could not reach. Jesus converted the inner man and gave the Holy Spirit as an indwelling guest in the soul to enlighten the mind and enkindle the heart for a lifetime. Christian baptism need never be repeated, though it might need to be remembered and its flames aroused.

John recognizes Jesus even when John is but a few months older in the womb of his mother, Elizabeth. He leaps for joy, and she is filled with the Holy Spirit (Lk 1:44). Jesus took over John's work when John was imprisoned. When John was beheaded by Herod, who feared John's criticism of his marriage would undermine his authority and enable his enemies to challenge Herod's reign, Jesus must have questioned his own future destiny. The death of John foreshadows the death of Jesus, and as they were united providentially in their birth, so they are united in standing for the truth and in giving their lives to God, the one the culmination of the Covenant of the Old Testament, the other the inauguration of the New Covenant for all eternity.

The Grand Reunion

With many dozen chapels on the campus of Notre Dame, one will find many versions of the Stations of the Cross in many materials. In the crypt of the Basilica the Stations are engravings with the inscriptions in French. In the Basilica proper, the stations are large oil paintings. In Sorin Hall the stations are fired clay bas-reliefs, and around the edge of St. Joseph Lake the outdoor stations are bronze. Our Lady of Fatima displays the stations in mosaics along a winding trail. Each residence hall has its own Stations of the Cross in whatever style might have been installed. You can well suspect a church is a Catholic Church if you find the Stations of the Cross. Whatever happened to the many characters in this Passion Narrative? And whatever happened to all of the Notre Dame alumni and alumnae who never appear in the Alumni Notes in the "Notre Dame Magazine"? Good questions.

WE WONDER WHAT HAPPENED to our classmates, to our neighborhood friends who moved away, to stories begun but never finished to our knowing. Have you ever wondered what happened to the many characters in the

153

Gospel? What happened to the Samaritan woman at the well, with whom Jesus spoke so long and well, or Pilate's wife who held Jesus in high regard? What happened to Lazarus raised from the dead, but destined to die again? Did he laugh at death's ravages, as the playwright Eugene O'Neill imagined? And what happened to the daughter of Jairus and the son of the widow of Nain, both raised from the dead by Jesus, but someday to die again. How long did they live and what did they do with their re-suscitated life? What of Nicodemus and Joseph of Ari-mathea, friends of Jesus in his death, and cryptic-be-lievers while he lived? And what of the several women in the gospels who followed Jesus, and the many wom-en who stood at the foot of his cross? What of the Cen-turion who alone proclaims, "Truly this was the Son of God," at the Calvary death of Jesus? Legend suggests he was the same Centurion who said: "I am not wor-thy that you enter my house, but say but the word" (Mt 8:8). What of his son and on and on? The woman who is healed of her hemorrhage upon touching the hem of his garment when Jesus is on the way to raise up the daugh-ter of Jairus is thought by legend to be Veronica, the woman who wipes the face of Jesus with a cloth on his road to Calvary. And what of all our Notre Dame grad-uates throughout the world, whose lives were so touched by Our Lady's University? We would love to know, and some day we shall know and come together at that grand reunion we call the "Communion of Saints."

Mary Magdalene
and the Many Marys

College dating has never been easy. In earlier times women were not students on the campus, and that alone made dating a challenge, even with women students across the street at St. Mary's College. Insecurities all round in both genders complicated dating rituals. In the contemporary scene with men and women side by side on campus, dating still falls into a no-man's and no woman's land between friendships and "friends with benefits" that engage the body but not the heart. Dating as courtship continues, of course, but sorting it all out has never been easy. In the musical, "Godspell," Mary of Magdala sings a poignant lament about her attraction to Jesus of Nazareth. "I don't know how to love him" expresses her dilemma. She recognizes he is not like other men she has known in wanting one way or the other to exploit her, and she does not want to employ her own manipulation and self-defenses in matters of the heart, when she has finally found a love that exceeds anything known of love in her life before. This Mary is not sure what to do. She is not alone.

IF POSTERITY IS to remember you, then you might want to have a good picture of yourself taken, and you need a biographer with some sympathy for you. Mary Magdalene had neither. Later generations portray her as the penitent sinner of the Lukan story of the sinful woman who washes the feet of Jesus with her tears and dries them with her hair. (Lk 7: 44-50) Her sin, one should note, is quite unnamed, but a woman who lets her long hair down in public may suggest a prostitute. Just after the story of this unnamed woman with the unnamed sin, Luke speaks of Mary Magdalene, from whom Jesus cast out seven devils. Mary from the town of Magdala along the shore of the Sea of Galilee need not be the woman who washes the feet of Jesus and likely is not. Her "seven devils" are shorthand for a generic mental illness, from which Jesus cured her. She became one of the women in the entourage that followed Jesus and provided for him from their means (Lk 8:3).

Mary Magdalene more recently has been portrayed as "the" woman friend, perhaps spouse, perhaps mother of a child, and surely involved with Jesus. "The Last Temptation of Christ" movie and "The DaVinci Code" book and movie excited conspiracy seekers around the world. What the Gospel says of a love affair is naught. What the Gospel does say of Mary Magdalene is routinely overlooked. Mary Magdalene is the apostle to the apostles, the first one who met the risen Jesus when she was grieving at his tomb and thinking she was talking to the gardener. Mary of Magdala was at the foot of the cross. Jesus calls her by name in the empty-tomb scene.

She would cling to his feet and bring him back into this world. She loved him; he loved her. The rest is speculation and sometimes titillation.

The women in the Gospels are quite wonderful. Mary of Nazareth, the mother of Jesus and the Mother of God, is the only human being who knows Jesus from his conception to his crucifixion, from the womb to the tomb. Mary of Bethany, sister to Martha and Lazarus, whom Jesus loved, poured precious ointment on the feet of Jesus and dried them with her hair (Jn 12:3-8). In Mark's gospel, in perhaps a parallel story, an unnamed woman anoints the head of Jesus, and to her and her alone does he speak these remarkable words: "Wherever the Gospel is preached, this story shall be told in memory of her" (Mk 14:9).

Three episodes of anointing of Jesus in anticipation of his crucifixion and death are recorded -- the unknown woman in Mark, the unknown woman in Luke, Mary of Bethany in John. Is there one woman, one story, but told three ways by three evangelists? Mary of Magdala is not one of these three, but neither is she the prostitute who becomes in legend the repentant sinner. What we see in all of the women in these Gospel accounts is this: love extravagant, expressive, bold, that counts not the cost, that gives all for love, that tells of their love before death intervenes, that bears the grief of impending loss, and that leaves the rest of us quite breathless at their ardor so richly displayed.

The Little Ones

If you ever wondered whether there was sinfulness on the campus of Notre Dame, you need but lift the "Campus Manual of Bad Behavior," named Du Lac. *We expect mistakes and even sin among college-age students. After all they are young. After all college is a place where most mistakes do not have irremediable consequences. The campus is a time and place to learn in a safe environment. When the students or the young in education are themselves victims, however, something has gone very wrong. Scandal may always be with us, but it is never less than shocking. In the youth of springtime, the green leaves are unfurled unspoiled by insect bites or the dust and dirt of a long hot summer. Young and innocent always colors the campus, even though we know that one of the things that must be learned in college years is that trust has to be somewhat tentative. Street sense must be learned. Not everyone can be trusted, and not only students make mistakes and need to recognize they are sinful.*

WHEN THE GOSPEL SPEAKS of the "little ones," who have been abused (Lk 17:2), one may well think of the scandal

of child abuse throughout the ages and predominantly
perpetrated by family members. At this time, however,
one thinks of clergy sexual abuse in the Catholic Church
in America. It is a big story, long concealed, with record
money settlements, and media coverage both thorough
and sometimes more than thorough. The 2007 settle-
ment in Los Angeles reached six hundred million dollars. Surely that sum of money is a lot of money, and yet
divided into sixty million Catholics in this country the
sum is but ten dollars. Divided into the fifty-year pe-
riod covered in the lawsuits, that sum turns out to be
pennies per person per week, even if one factors in population growth. Money, however, is not the real issue:
"better that a millstone was hung around their neck"
(Mk 9:42). We barely can contemplate in our imagination what harm can be done in abuse of the young. We
expected so much more of our faith, so much more moral integrity in our priests, so much more protection and
care of those most vulnerable by our bishops. The damage may never be undone in this world.

And then there is the cover-up by the bishops, some
of it venal and arrogant, some of it well intentioned and
even compassionate. Were one to learn that a husband
or wife, brother or sister, mother or father, was involved
in child abuse, who would first think to turn them in to
the police? Would most of us try to bring them to professional help, hoping for a change of behavior, rather
than immediately turning them over to the penal code?
Putting a parent in jail might even sound like a different kind of child abuse. Is there no middle way? Might

we not move to another location in hope of a fresh start and a clean outcome? And yet, by law, we should immediately turn the accused over to the police. Bad judgment is never excusable, but sometimes it is understandable. Nonetheless the law rightly protects the innocent, especially the young, and the law when not followed causes irreparable damage to children and does not even truly protect the perpetrator of what might well be compulsion and addiction well mixed with human tragedy and sinfulness. One wants to weep for everyone involved, but for the children most of all.

Jepthah's Daughter

When Father Hesburgh passes from this life, I expect a very large memorial funeral at Notre Dame. The longer he lives, however, the smaller the number of the friends and associates of his life who will be able to attend his passing. If a student dies suddenly at Notre Dame, there is likely to be just the opposite mourning. That student lived with all of us and was so alive just the day before. No matter one's age, we have here no lasting city. "Sic transit gloria mundi" is an ancient saying that reminds us that all of us and all we accomplish is subject to the passage of time. Fame is fickle and all lives remain unfinished symphonies. The "Salve Regina" so often sung at Notre Dame says it well. This life is a "vale of tears" and we pray that "this our exile" conclude in our death that is our birth into an everlasting life where "death will be no more" (Rv 21:4).

ONE OF THE HORROR STORIES of the Hebrew Scriptures remains the tale of Jepthah (see Judges 11). The story in short is this. Jephtah is a petty king at war, who promises the almighty God that he will sacrifice the first person he lays eyes on, were he to be assisted to defeat the enemy.

After his victory he returns home, and his eyes alight first upon his one and only child, a daughter of marriage age, whom he now believes he must kill in sacrifice to a God whom he believes would want him to keep his word at any cost. The young woman does not protest or rebel, but accepts her destiny to die in sacrifice. She asks only for a short leave of absence to go with her maidens into a place of solitude in order to mourn her virginity. She might have been married and gave birth to children, whose children and children's children could fill the earth. Her life will now be barren and seemingly futile and in vain.

Her trust in trimming one's dreams to God's will and accepting without lament or complaint a road that can only be compared with a way of the cross, displays her in the story as beautiful and serene, whereas her father appears coarse and troubled. In the end, the horror is redeemed by a lovely maiden who lays down her life willingly, much as Jesus redeems a world where such horrors are not unknown, by willingly giving his body to the nails of a cross of painful death. How strange that the horror and the love can co-penetrate. Quite wonderful how a story of father and child can both chill and warm us so. "Blessed are those who mourn, for they shall be consoled" (Mt 5:4).

The Judas Story

Practical jokes that go wrong can happen and have happened on the Notre Dame campus. Someone gets hurt, either physically or emotionally, and that outcome may not have been intended. Candid photos mounted on Internet sites can devastate the victim of "a joke." The tape recorder placed under the bed can ruin someone's life, because the betrayal is so keen. Many betrayals in our life are real and some are imagined. We learn early in our education that not everything is what it appears to be, nor everyone the person we thought him or her to be. The story of Judas might be a moral paradigm of how we can get it wrong. To understand all is to forgive all. Some mistakes are just that—well-intentioned efforts that went horribly wrong. The apostle, Jude, is regarded as the patron of hopeless causes, and there is a statue of him tucked in the lawn between the Basilica and Corby Hall on campus. Judas and Jude are easily confused, and no doubt Judas was thought to be the true hopeless cause. And yet, God might really write straight with crooked lines.

RASH JUDGMENT IS a rush to judgment. Rash judgment is pre-judice, that is, judging beforehand, before the issue is ripe for judgment. "The verdict first and then the evidence," as the Queen says to Alice in Wonderland. Perhaps we have concluded that Judas, who betrayed Jesus and then went out and hung himself, is somehow a case of despair beyond the reach of forgiveness. I am going to argue that Judas may have received a bad rap.

Truth to tell, we all love to hate a villain – whether it is the Yankees in baseball, Notre Dame in football, Hitler in World War II, or Al Queda in the global village. We need a demon, whose guilt is beyond dispute and beyond our guilt, so that we can feel relatively good about ourselves. For many centuries many Christians could paint the Jews of the Gospels as villains, or the Muslims in the Holy Land. There were always minorities, the outsiders, the gays, the witches, the scapegoats of human culture whom we must find a way to blame and to unload our own accumulated and often unrecognized guilt. And then, for Christians, every Easter season we could lay it on Judas. I want to paint a picture of Judas without projection of our own troubles.

First of all, Judas was hand-picked by Jesus, who could read the human heart. He surely was not moral trash, though I do not wish to say he was beyond sin or grave moral failure. His heart must have been true, though his behavior may have gone amiss. To betray Jesus for thirty pieces of silver, a small sum, makes little sense, especially if, as John's Gospel tells us, Judas helped himself to the common purse. He may have been dishonest, but would he likely be a traitor unto death of a man as good as Jesus was to everyone. And if Judas was a scumbag villain, why ever would he return the silver to the priests and then in a despairing remorse go out and hang himself? And if Jesus knew he was a traitorous villain, why did Jesus walk into such a trap when he could avoid it? Why keep Judas at the supper table, why predict betrayal, and why allow the kiss of greeting, unless what was going on was more than meets the eye?

Simon the Zealot was one of Jesus' chosen apostles. He was a Zionist of his day, a religious theocrat, who wanted the Roman Empire gone from Israel and the people of God politically beholden to God alone. Suppose Judas was a Zealot as well. His hopes and dreams were with Jesus as the new Moses, no doubt the Messiah to come, the God-anointed one who would set his people free. Jesus, however, seemed so laid back and showed so little political fervor. Let us suppose Judas thought he could light Jesus' fire. Were Jesus arrested, he would have to break out of jail to continue his preaching and healing. That rebellion would be the spark that would unite the people behind Jesus in order to oust the Romans. No one could bind Jesus who raised the dead, walked on water, and calmed the storm. And then it all went horribly wrong. Jesus did not resist. He went like a lamb to slaughter. Judas suffered the despair of someone who might pull a practical joke that all unintentionally led to someone's death. It was not supposed to result tragically in the crucifixion of Jesus, but in the liberation of Israel. In despair, Judas throws the money of no

consequence to him back at the officials, and in overwhelming remorse for what he had done to Jesus, whom
he loved in his own way, he proceeds to hang himself.
Not exactly a villain, this Judas, and no saint either. He
may not be someone to hate but someone to pity, and a
lesson to us all that we cannot make peace with violence
and force. The end never does justify the means. However noble the end, manipulative or devious means will
not in the end bring about justice and peace. The cross
endured, however, just may save a sinful world.

The Widow Of Nain

Some of our students may be the son or daughter of a widowed mother (or father). Some of our students may be the only son or the only daughter in the family. Many of our students come from one-parent families. First funerals can surprise a college student who has heretofore not encountered death. The death of a grandparent or a parent can overwhelm, and the quick support of the Notre Dame campus is quite remarkable. When a student dies the compassionate response is heartfelt. Some students and the rector from the residence hall may well travel to the funeral, and on campus there will be prayers and a memorial mass. Mary was a mother with an only child, an only son, much like the widow of Nain in the Gospel story. She knew. Even worst, she saw what happened to her son who died all too young and all too cruelly. Life is not fair, and yet God's care is never absent to us.

DID JESUS LAUGH AND CRY? He must have, if he was human, but the gospels do not record many tears nor laughter. Jesus' first encounter with death in the Gospel of John occurs when his friend, Lazarus, suddenly dies. Jesus wept at they led him to the grave (Jn 11:35).

Jesus also wept over Jerusalem (Lk 19:41) as he looked upon it as a mother bird who would want to gather her chicks in the shelter of her wings. Jesus told the women of Jerusalem not to weep for him as he carried his cross toward Calvary (Lk 23:28), but to weep for themselves in the coming annihilation of Jerusalem. Jesus tells the widow mother of Nain not to weep for her only son, who has died and is about to be buried (Lk 7:13). Was Jesus thinking of his own mother in a future scene of a widowed mother whose only son was about to be taken down from a cross? Perhaps so; we know he raises the young man to life. He raises Lazarus to life. He raises the young daughter of Jairus to life. Jesus came to raise the dead.

What happens to us when we die? Are our souls without any body, even the attenuated or shadowy body of the shades of the underworld of antiquity. Even as we await the resurrection of the body and life everlasting on the last day, at the moment of our death do we not go to God as human, somehow a soul embodied, however incomplete our resurrection? Do not the saints dwell with God in heaven? And then, may we wonder if Lazarus wanted to return to this life on earth? Does the son of the widow of Nain receive a second chance at beatitude, and does the young innocent daughter of Jairus contract double jeopardy in her return to this life? Would we and should we ask our beloved dead to come back to us? Do we not die unto a better life? Are we not born into eternal life on the day we die, and should we not want to leave the sum of this earthly life? Jesus restored earthly life to but a few people in the Gospels, but he restored heavenly life to us one and all by his life and by his death. In his death and resurrection he was not called back to this life, and he told Mary Magdalene in the burial-garden that she was not to cling to him in his appearance to her. Jesus wept for the living as well as for the dead. Death is our passage to everlasting life, and that cannot be all bad.

The Lady On The Dome

*Students are not here for August 15th, the Feast of the
Assumption of Mary. The Golden Dome proclaims it
in the glimmer of late summer sun. The football team is
holding its pre-season practice. Residence-hall-staff are
lining up their orientation classes. The campus is all a
preparation, much as this life is a practice and a learning
for another more momentous life to come. In the Basilica of the Sacred Heart, two large stained glass windows
dominate the sanctuary where the nave and the transept
cross in the pattern of the cross of Christ. These two
beautiful wall-filling windows reveal the passage of the
Blessed Virgin Mary (Notre Dame) from the birth of the
Church at the descent of the Holy Spirit upon the apostles at Pentecost depicted in the east window to the great
window in the west, seen in the fading light of day, where
Mary lies on her death bed, surrounded by the Church
in the person of the twelve apostles. They minister in
prayer at her birth into eternal life. Her body would be
assumed into heaven in the anticipation of the fullness of
the resurrection, just as her first moment of conception in
this life was filled with the Holy Spirit in anticipation of
the redemption of Jesus Christ. From east to west, from*

170

morning to evening, from birth in this world to death that is birth to eternal life, we pass through the Church with the Mother of God, who has gone before us.

FAITH IN THE ASSUMPTION of Mary did not stem from the written scriptures. Nothing in the Gospels touches on her death. A vague reference in the Apocalypse has been cited – the woman who appears in the sky with the moon at her feet (Rv 12:1). That text, however, has been read many different ways. Tradition held that Mary was never buried. No one claims a tomb or a burial site for the Mother of God. Tradition, as the memory of the living community, held Mary assumed on high. No Church or shrine in Christendom claims to hold her body. There is no evidence of her bones, no relics that are credible. Mary simply disappeared. Some say she but fell asleep and woke in heaven. Most theologians conclude she must have died, because Jesus died, but that she was never separated from him. She who alone knew the Lord Jesus from birth to death was not to be denied the everlasting presence of her Son. Where he was, she would be. He rose from the dead and ascended into heaven. Mary went to "sleep" and was assumed into heaven from the sleep of death. Mary, who is fully one of us, stands for us, body and soul, with the Lord Jesus. She is the Holy Grail, the Mother of God, the Ark of the Covenant, the House of Gold. How could we imagine God the Father would allow the grave to ravage her body? It was God's only beloved son whom she bore into this world, creating his body from her own. Cardinal Newman thought it was impossible to acknowledge too much in praise and recognition of Mary. One might fail in wordings, and one Mariology may be better than another, but the dignity and loveliness of the mother of the Word made flesh can scarcely be exaggerated.

As I walked by chance in Cedar Grove Cemetery on one Assumption Day, I stopped by the monument of Alexis Coquillard. A very large plinth is raised over his bones. We bury our dead and protect their bones, for we cherish our belief in the resurrection of the body. Relics of the saints that were a speck of bone were held precious. One honored a piece of heaven, for these bones were sure to rise to glory. For such reasons the Church disregarded cremation until recently.

The Cedar Grove Cemetery Columbaria have just been completed. Dorms for the dead, they have been nicknamed. Just a bit of ashes, the remains of the body gathered up in a funeral urn, which can no longer support our misconception that the resurrection of the body is some kind of miraculous resuscitation of our dead body even when reduced to bare bones, much less ashes. Resurrection is a greater miracle than resuscitation. Our resurrection is a mystery beyond all logic. The mystery of the assumption of the Blessed Virgin Mary, body and soul, into everlasting life, foreshadows our own mysterious participation in that same life everlasting.

Wheat And Weeds

I have heard that the campus is a Catholic Disneyland, but I have never heard that Notre Dame is the Kingdom of God on earth or the Garden of Paradise. We know that there is a mixture of virtue and sin, of good and bad, of fair and unfair on this campus. We are in the world, even if we wish not to be of the world. No one here is without sin. Humility befits us and patience. We are an unfinished story. One has but to read the history of Notre Dame and the many-sided conflict between Fr. Edward Sorin, c.s.c, as founder of the university, and Fr. Basil Moreau, c.s.c., founder of the Congregation of Holy Cross, to recognize that our roots, our motives, our virtues and our vices are all entangled, and that only God in the end time will fully sort out our days. In the meantime, we bear each others' burdens, and we like to think at Notre Dame we do so with some humor and some willingness to carry more than our share on occasion. Who of us would write our autobiography today in just the same way we would have as a student at Notre Dame? Some weeds back then turned out to be wheat, and some wheat back then turned out to be weeds. We think we know what is good and what is bad for us, but we are not infallible judges of the providence of God.

HOW SHOULD WE TELL the wheat from the weeds, what we want to keep and what we want to throw away? A rose in a wheat field is a weed; wheat in a rose garden is a weed. What does not belong is a weed, but in our lives that is harder to see than in our plantings. God's providence prevails in our lives, and what belongs in it will enter in due time, and whatever enters will in due time be seen to belong in our lives. Surely we have all known the experience of mistaking our true friends. Those who seemed an enemy at one time may come to be recognized as a friend who told us hard truth we were not prepared to hear. Who once seemed a friend may prove in moments of crises or temptation to be no such thing. Time will tell seems good advice in sizing up what is truly good for us, and what we may conclude at the moment is God's will for us. God does write straight with crooked lines, and "for those who love God all things commingle unto good" (Rm 8: 28). As a young girl my mother was asked to spend an occasional weekend with her elderly uncle and aunt, who lived far from town in the swampy backwater of the bayous of Louisiana. There were no playmates and not much for a child to do. She resented the imposition and the boredom. In later years long after her elders had died and left her a share in the swamp, a great deal of oil money came her way and just when she most needed help. Coincidence perhaps, providence no doubt. Hard to know the wheat from the weeds, the

providence from the coincidence. Or maybe all is providential, were we to have eyes to see.

The Gospel parable of the weeds sown by the enemy
in a farmer's wheat field makes just this point. Wheat and
weeds are not only hard to distinguish at first, but their
roots are entwined and hard to separate. We may need to
allow both the good and the bad to coexist side by side,
because we cannot uproot the one without harming the
other. Our virtues and our vices are intertwined. For
example, those persons most compassionate may lack
fortitude. Those persons most courageous may lack em-
pathy. The quick often blunder; the cautious often are
too late. Look before you leap, but he who hesitates is
lost. God's ways are not our ways, and what we thought
weed and what we thought wheat may in the ways of God
surprise us.

Transfiguration

In a difficult football game, pundits sometimes announce that the moment is "gut-check time." Does one team want to win so badly that they will pay any price in pain to win? I suppose there are many moments that call for such courage in college years. Job interviews come to mind, and marriage proposals to be made or accepted come to mind. Broken hearts, room-pick desolations, academic failures – there are inevitable moments of crisis on any college campus. What God is doing with us, and what we are doing with ourselves tend to blur. There are moments of faith and moments of doubt. What is certain remains that we are changed, and to have lived is to have changed often.

AUGUST 6TH, THE FEAST of the Transfiguration and the annual anniversary of the explosion of the first atom bomb above the city of Hiroshima coincide. I was then in the seventh grade with Sister Maureen, the nun-teacher whom I most loved. We practiced atomic bomb attacks with classroom drills that taught us to seek shelter under our wooden desks stained with black writing ink. I cannot separate the Transfiguration of Jesus, whose face

176

shone as the sun, with the day a city of living human beings was incinerated in a flash of blinding light.

Come back to Notre Dame. Come back to your class
in theology, or Bible, or homily spoken in Church on
this day. What did you long ago think of what happened
on Mount Tabor? Here is what I once thought. Jesus,
who all along was super-man in a mere human tunic,
decided to give his three closest friends – Peter, John,
and James --- a glimpse at what and who he really was
underneath his disguise. He stepped out of his human
body for a time and let his divinity transfigure his humanity. He was dazzling as the sun.

No longer do I believe in such a big-bang miracle
on Tabor. I do believe in a miracle, and even a bigger
one than the creation of the sun and the other stars. Jesus was at this moment of his life afraid his enemies
were about to pounce on him. He took his friends on
an overnight retreat of prayer for the strength and support to go on to Jerusalem. They fell asleep; Jesus prayed
all night to the God of Moses and Elijah. Jesus came
to accept the wisdom of the biblical accounts of how
God works miracles through failure and suffering. In
the morning, Jesus' face shone with this mystical union
with God. Gloom and depression were gone. "What happened to you?" the three disciples then say. Jesus found
his courage and his deepest faith on Tabor. Peter, James,
and John slept through his dark night of the soul, as
they did again in the Garden of Gethsemani, when Tabor was tested against the pending and boding horrors

of Calvary. There too angels of heaven came to him in prayer. The real revelation of Jesus in all his glory would be on Mount Calvary, not on Mount Tabor. The miracle greater than the creation is the mystery of the cross.

Loaves And Fishes

If an army moves on its stomach, no doubt a college campus moves on its stomach. Food is consumed in plentiful amounts, and the pursuit of good food at a good price is a college past-time. Two large dining halls at Notre Dame feed crowds in the thousands. The student union is dotted with food vendors, and smaller lunch spots are found in many of the more populated campus buildings. No one goes hungry at Notre Dame. Tail-gate parties, Dine-out menus and pizza deliveries run day and night. Food trucks of various descriptions ply the roads with their culinary goods. Leftovers from the dining halls feed the Homeless Shelter in South Bend and beyond. Food for the mind, food for the soul, food for the body – that may sum up college life.

CONSIDER THE STORY told in all four gospels of the multiplication of the loaves and fishes to feed a crowd of thousands. Spectacular would be the miracle of seven loaves and two fishes become a basket that never runs out of food. From next to nothing, more loaves and fishes emerge in great quantity. It would be a physical miracle that dazzles. Another reading has been

179

suggested, a reading not described in the gospel narrative, though one may maintain the gospel narrative is not a videotape of an event but rather a deep understanding of an event. Suppose the videotape, which we are not given, played out like this. People traveling in the wilderness far from home and town carried food and water for the journey. Some emergency food was used only as a last resort, and suppose Jesus and his disciples gave up all they had with them and shared it. Others might do the same, and if everyone gave everything they had, there would be no want or hunger in all the world. The conversion of the human heart to a self-giving generosity might not be as spectacular as bread loaves appearing out of nowhere in a basket, but a change of human hearts is a spiritual miracle, far more difficult even for God to bring about than baking bread. Conversion of heart remains the greatest miracle on earth, though not the most spectacular. What purpose would abundance of food ever have if not to lead people to recognize the hand that feeds us all and the earth and universe besides? In the end the gospel story is not all about matter, but rather all about soul. The story is not all about food on earth, but all about the bread of God to feed our hearts. The greatest miracle in the world is the conversion of the human heart. God created the world out of nothing, so claims the Judeo-Christian faith. Nothingness offered no resistance to God. Human freedom, however, can deter God's grace, and the sinner begins in a negative cast of mind that is resistant. Conversion is God's greatest miracle of creation, changing a hard heart into a soft heart, a loveless heart into a loving heart, all the while respecting the true freedom of soul of the human being. Conversion is not usually a spectacular miracle. It is more hidden and more quiet, like the birth of the savior in Bethlehem that changed the whole world.

The Good Samaritan

The Center for Social Concerns, serendipitously named CSC Center, has been a great success at Notre Dame. Even as I write these words its new home nearby the Hesburgh Library is under construction. The old NBC Television studio, which subsequently housed the Center for Social Concerns for many years, was torn down to make room for the new "Church-Life" building. A majority of Notre Dame students give volunteer help during their college years. Many undergraduates undertake summer projects sponsored by the Alumni Association in various cities. Upon graduation about ten percent of Notre Dame students give a year of volunteer service in some form. Motives perhaps vary. Helping those in need surely predominates, even if there may be self-interest. A generous love of God and the poor blends well. Service and faith, faith and service; they belong together. The Scriptures have a quite unique take on that tension. " 'Lord, when did we see you hungry or thirsty or a stranger or naked or sick or in prison, and not did not take care of you?' Then he will answer them, 'Truly I tell you, just as you did not do it to one of the least of these, you did not do it to me' " (Mt 25:44-45).

WITH THE PASSAGE of the years many judgments made in our youth and student days are revised. Some things that were right then seem wrong now, and what then might have been neglected now may be prized. We change because we think about it all with more wisdom and experience. There is a biblical story that tells this lesson most profoundly. On the road to Jericho, a man is robbed and abandoned, left wounded by the roadside. A Priest and then a Levite walk by and cross to the other side of the road. Their living depends on not being judged ritually unclean, and if they touch a man very likely dead, they will be ruled unclean. Better not to take a chance. A Samaritan coming by does stop, and he rescues the wounded man and cares for him at personal cost. Samaritans were mostly despised by Jews. Jesus says that this Samaritan recognized his neighbor, and every human being in need is the neighbor we must love.

Right following this parable in Luke, friends of Jesus in Bethany, in whose home he likely stayed during the festivals when Jerusalem was crowded with visitors, are sitting down to a luncheon. Martha is cooking and complaining that her sister Mary is sitting idle at the feet of Jesus and listening to him. She should help in the kitchen, but Jesus replies to Martha that listening to his words is even more important than feeding the hungry.

In truth, however, charity remains always more important than prayer or listening, but Luke juxtaposes the Samaritan who rescues and Mary who listens at the feet of Jesus to tell us something crucial about loving. Unless you find time to pray, to listen, to contemplate, to hold to an inner spiritual life, you will not recognize who is the neighbor to be loved. Nor will one recognize who is wounded, disregarded, and how to help in the right way and with a self-giving motivation. One will not love as Jesus loved, laying down his life, unless one has sat at his feet and listened prayerfully to the very heart of Jesus, which is God's heart and God's love, to be embodied us.

The Mercy: A Reprise

IN THIS ESSAY I REVIEW several key insights into God's mercy and our conversion to mercy in our lives. Dear reader, forgive me the repetition. I could have cut this essay altogether, but I am hoping that you will find a reprise valuable, because I have found mercy so very pivotal and so very precious.

In college years, if not sooner, many of us have been given a second chance. Mistakes made by the young are more easily forgiven. Juvenile justice is based on the fact that teens do not yet know fully what they are doing. Jesus' words on the cross are always a propos: "Father, forgive them, they know not what they do" (Lk 23:34). With school-age students, even police records are expunged, crimes bargained to misdemeanors, and all in an attempt to give a young person a break, a chance at a clean start, a second chance, a forgiveness that is a mercy.

Later in life we may also receive mercy, a second chance, a reconciliation, a forgiveness. When my older brother, whom I hardly knew at all, was dying of brain cancer, I went to help him at his home in Louisiana. He told me: "I did not understand and I did not care." He hurt my feelings, but he told the truth. Days and weeks passed. Toward the end of his days as he lay in bed I was so tired that I put my head down on his hand for a pillow. It was then that he kissed me, and I knew that he knew I tried my best as did he. It was a mercy and a mutual forgiveness. I would grieve his death, but even more I grieved the brother whom I never had until the mercy at the end.

Forgiveness is not about God changing. Mercy is not about God being angry with our sin and then, because we repent, God relents. That is a description of human forgiveness not even at its best. The injured party decides to accept the sinner more or less back into good graces. Not so with God. God is infinitely happy always, and our sins do not diminish God's happiness. God pities how our sins diminish our happiness and that of others. In God's mercy it is our hard and ruthless hearts that change to soft and compassionate hearts. It is our unhappiness and anger that must change, and the way we know we have allowed ourselves to receive God's forgiveness remains that we recognize God's forgiveness truly received has melted our hearts. We are not the same after we have been forgiven. God has not changed; we have changed. God is love; in mercy we receive God's love and we change. Of the woman who washes the feet of Jesus with her tears and dries them with her hair Jesus says: "Therefore, I tell you, her sins, which were many, have been forgiven; hence she has shown great love" (Lk 7: 47). The woman's love follows the mercy of God, not the mercy of God follows the woman's love.

In Luke's parable, both the prodigal son and the elder righteous son misunderstand the love of their father, who is the prodigal father. His love is lavish; his mercy is God's unconditional love. Neither the bad behavior of the prodigal son nor the good behavior of the dutiful son accounts for their father's love. Sin does not lose us God's love; virtue does not earn us God's love. Divine love is gratuitous and unconditional. We are loved because we are his sons and daughters. We always were and always will be the beloved children of God and the everlasting friends of Jesus. God's love is never dependent on our behavior.

Mercy, however, does not overlook the consequences of sin. The sinner is the first victim and then many others connected to the sinner. To some degree we are all connected in our humanity and in the communion of sinners as well as saints. We belong to each other, like it or not. Mercy opposes sin, because sin harms self and others. When Jesus forgives sin, however, he exacts no vengeance. He covers our shame and deflects our blame. Jesus says on the cross: "I do not hold your hurting me against you. Think no more about it. You are forgiven freely and completely." Christian forgiveness says in effect: "I who am sinned against wish you to carry no burden of shame or blame. You have hurt yourself most of all, and you must recognize in sorrow what you have done to yourself and to others. You will grieve, but you owe me nothing. I grant you amnesty, full pardon. You will have to suffer your own recognition. You will have to make some kind of peace and restoration with those you have hurt by your sins, not because it is demanded of you by payback, but because demanded by a thankful and growing love in you. Mercy is the heart of forgiveness. To forgive a debt is but to cancel it. Banks do that when bankruptcy is declared. Mercy does more than cancel the debt of sin; mercy removes the burden within. Mercy wishes there to be neither shame nor blame. Mercy is the gratuitous and unconditional love that is God's love.

When Jesus washed the feet of his disciples, he took away any shame they may have ever had. He did not find them an embarrassment. He knew their weakness and betrayal. He loved them and found them washed clean, precisely because he so loved them. When Jesus walked through the locked door of the inner room where the disciples were imprisoned in fearful shame and blame, he took the shame away and said to them, "Peace be with you" (Jn 20: 21), and he took the blame away when he said to them, "whose sins you shall forgive are forgiven them" (Jn 20: 23). No shame, no blame, nothing but the mercy of God.

The Sacrament of Confession and Reconciliation is not the only way God forgives sins. The sacrament, however, may be a help in amplifying the mercy of God. How else to hear the voice of God saying that one is loved and forgiven, if not to confess to another human being who is a minister of God's love? How better to choose a merciful confidant than to choose a ordained stranger pledged to silence and to compassion? How else to apologize to the human community at large, if not to open to one chosen by the community to represent them and to give mercy in their place and in their name? Confession at times is a burden, but most of the time confession is a mercy.

CHAPTER SIX
ENGAGEMENTS

Marriage

On almost every weekend of the year, weddings in the Basilica of the Sacred Heart at Notre Dame come one after the other. Reservations are made months and more in advance, and only current faculty and staff, alums of the university, or parishioners of the local parish are able to celebrate a wedding on campus. They come and go in horse-drawn carriages, in trolleys, in hummers, in stretch-limos, in buses. Photos in the Grotto seem de rigeur. Bridesmaids and Best Men are dressed out. Flowers and choirs are ample. Expenses are extravagant often enough. As a young priest I was often a tad struck by the bride's beauty and goodness. As an older priest, I know that marriage is a Christian vocation that involves both joy and the cross, and to give a young couple a joyous and lavish send-off may seem the least the family can do.

TOLSTOY'S NOVEL, *War and Peace*, touches on all dimensions of human life and death. There is only one event missing; there is no wedding. Perhaps he thought the real meaning of a marriage was indescribable. Perhaps Church weddings were too elaborate and too religious. Had he written of a wedding, I would have been pleased had he included the wedding homily. For many years in Roman Catholic weddings in the United States there was a set homily in the ceremony. It was a unique blend of the romantic and the realistic, an awareness that grace builds on nature, and a deep understanding that there is no other way of life or way of happiness that is not at heart a self-giving love and also a way of the cross. Self-sacrifice and love go together. I give the text of that homily below:

My dear friends: you are about to enter into a union which is most sacred and most serious. It is most sacred, because established by God himself, most serious, because it will bind you together for life in a relationship so close and so intimate, that it will profoundly affect your whole future. That future, with its hopes and disappointments, its successes and its failures, its pleasures and its pains, its joys and its sorrows, is now hidden from your eyes: yet you know that these elements are part of every life and should be expected in your own. And so, not knowing what is before you, you take each other for better or for worse, for richer or for poorer, in sickness and in health, until death.

Truly, then, these words are most serious. It is a beautiful tribute to your undoubted faith in eath other that, recognizing their full import, you are nevertheless so willing and ready to pronounce them. And because these words involve such solemn obligations, it is most fitting that you rest the security of your wedded life upon the great principles of self-sacrifice. And so you begin your married life with the voluntary and complete surrender of your individual lives in the interest of that deeper and wider life which you are to have in common. Henceforth you belong entirely to each other: You will be one in mind, one in heart, and one in affections. And whatever sacrifices you may hereafter be required to make for the preservation of this mutual life, always make them generously. Sacrifice is usually difficult and irksome. Only love can make it easy; and perfect love can make it a joy. We are willing to give in proportion as we love. And when love is perfect, the sacrifice is complete. God so loved the world that he gave his only begotten Son; and the Son so loved us that he gave himself for our salvation. Greater love than this no one has, than to lay down one's life for one's friends.

No greater blessing can come upon you and your married life than pure conjugal love, loyal and true to the end. May, then, this love with which you join your hands and hearts today, never fail, but grow deeper and stronger as the years go on. And if true love and the unselfish spirit of perfect sacrifice guide your every action, you can expect the greatest measure of earthly happiness that may be allotted to humans in this vale of tears. The rest is in the hands of God. Now will God be wanting to your needs: he will pledge you the lifelong support of his graces in the holy sacrament you are now going to receive. (*Author unknown*)

Divorce

Divorces, separations, single-parents, gay and lesbian marriages, all suggest that we have some issues about what commitments are valued and perhaps what commitments are possible. College students find it difficult to make a binding commitment with their lives. They live in a world where they are burdened with so many choices, so many roads, which if taken, cut off so many roads not taken. There is a certain paralysis because choices remain so abundant and theory about commitment so confused. The example of family and friends may or may not help to bind oneself to promises with but a hope of future happiness. "Promise Keepers" may be at heart patriarchal, but they do focus on the problem. Can we keep our promises? Can we commit to anyone or anything, for better or for worse, and unto death do us part?

ALL OF US KNOW of someone whose marriage ended in divorce. Most of us know someone in our family or close friends who share that same sorrow. Once upon a time divorce was unacceptable, and even kings-to-be must abdicate to marry a divorcée. Religious people shunned to some degree those who put asunder what God had joined. The sheer number of divorces and the good example of those we know in fruitful second marriages have neutralized divorce in our day. We accept divorce. We are not exactly happy, and no divorce was ever altogether happy. A dream died; a hope in a love bigger than human love falters. Some people hardly recover from a divorce; it is a wound that never quite heals. Time covers all sorrow, but when the weather is rainy, broken bones, though mended, yet remind us of back then.

I try to imagine a friendly divorce. I know of a few couples who talk to each other kindly, and even take care of the other in times of illness or emergency. They share the lives of their children with pride and move together without rancor. The love that was was real love. It has not died, even though they came to know they could not happily live together. We call it incompatibility and might rightly claim no-fault divorce.

Why could not the Churches, who uphold lifelong marriage, also allow separation? Could we not have a modest ceremony in Church in the afternoon, when the light is failing, that allows him and her to walk away with a blessing upon them by those who care to attend them? Could there be a blessing upon their future ways and deeply held hopes that God's love goes with us whatever paths we tread -- even on separate ways in this world that converge again only in the eternal life to come? Would we not pour oil thereby on the wound of divorce, instead of salt? Would we not take the wounded man or woman by the side of the road to the Inn that is the Church, and say what we all along intended: "Take care of her until I return; take care of him until I return" ? We are committed to take care of each other within divorce, despite divorce, in hope and trust that God writes straight with crooked lines, and for those who love God all things commingle together for good. That divine providence includes divorce, and most particularly when judged to be the last resort of good-hearted spouses who can see no other way, we could stand with them, who ask us all to try to understand and never to abandon them.

Passing On The Faith

Why do parents pay a good deal of money for a Catholic education, if their children have already distanced themselves from the faith of their parents? Do we hope the school can do what home could not accomplish – pass on the faith? Some families have noticed that their children who went to universities tended to lose their faith, and their children that ended their education in high school tended to keep close to home and especially to their parental faith. Other parents complain that there is no truth in advertising when Catholic universities claim to give a Catholic education. A faculty that is not pre-dominantly one of educated and committed Catholics, and a curriculum that requires only a couple of courses in religion or theology leads to nothing much of vibrant Catholic education. A secular university might offer as much through its Newman Center and its Religious Studies Department. In short, we do not seem to be doing well in passing on the faith to the next generation. I will say this of Notre Dame. Anyone who seeks or wants a Catholic education can and will receive a superb one on this campus. Resources galore are here, but they must be pursued, and they can also be avoided.

PARENTS WANT TO GIVE their children the best home, the best care, and the best education. They would even give their life to save their child's life, were that asked of them. Alas, what is often most precious to parents can be most difficult to give their children. Ideals, ethics, values, faith in God, and devotion to Church cannot be passed on to one's children with any guarantee they will be embraced in ways one can see.

For Catholic parents it can be a great sadness to see their children no longer attend Sunday mass. Who knows what they believe? Only God knows. They surely do not believe what their parents have believed. Perhaps this is the place to begin to comprehend that our children are not our own, and never have been. God loves them and courts their trust even more than we. And only God knows their heart from the inside, understands their thoughts, reads their intent, and graciously woos them unbeknownst, yet with a sovereign providence. What God wills, God gets. What God pursues, God captures. In theory, one can outrun God, but do you really think it is easily or often accomplished?

The apple does not fall far from the tree, and accordingly the faith and values of children reflect in the long run what they were taught and experienced at home. When home is not always good example, children may have taken that experience to heart as well. And yet, the good will and the effort of parents who are not perfect will be recognized and eventually appreciated. When children become parents themselves and must decide with what values and what faith will they bring up their children and embody in their own lives, a latent faith often emerges, much to everyone's surprise.

Bad example of Christian life and bad argument for belief in God generates much of what passes as unbelief in a younger generation. Belief is a very private and mysterious matter in the end, and perhaps God alone knows the depth of our faith. Those who use religious language with ease should not be presumptuous, and those who avoid religious language and practice need not despair. "Your God is too small" is a saying that always applies. Moreover, we do not discover God all by ourselves. We need a community of faith; we need some "church," whether we recognize that truth or not. Paul's conversion was quick and Augustine' conversion gradual. Peter was forgiven after public sin and failure. Jesus said of the pagan Roman Centurion that he had not "found such faith in all of Israel" (Lk 7: 9). We need to stay tuned. God is not finished with us yet, nor with our children.

Priest As Memory Of The Church

Someone in every family is keeper of the stories. Another person may be collector of the photographs. We try to remember what the family has endured and what accomplished. We try to pass on who we are, and where we came from, and even what is expected in the future. There is an historian in all of us. The priests and brothers of Holy Cross on the Notre Dame campus may well be such a continuity. In some ways they are the glue that holds the long story together. The Congregation of Holy Cross, as founders whose lives were lived and exhausted here, may well deserve to be called the "heartbeat of Notre Dame." They know where the bodies are buried. They know the good times and the bad, and they have shared with students, faculty, and staff moments of joy and sorrow, of marriage and birth, of life and of death. History is not a record of all that happened, but only of all that happened that someone thought worth preserving with some kind of record in writing, photograph, oral tradition, or whatever ways and means. The miracle of Notre Dame, as the miracle of the Church, might well be simply its survival and its flourishing.

I LIKE TO THINK of the priest as "memory of the Church." Our roots reach back into the Scriptures of millennia ago. We try to remember where we have been, what we suffered, what we learned, what went wrong, and what went right. Pastoral experience does accumulate in the Church. The past is no infallible guide to the future, but surely it should be remembered. The past might even be the right place to start if we want to change course in the future. The priest should add pastoral experience to a theological education. Surely the priest can give insight into where we have been, where we are now as a people of God on the road, and where we are going as our final destination. Amnesia is the constant threat to the spiritual life. We forget who we are, what we have received, and what hopes we entertain if we would but claim them. We forget what God has done for us, what God even now, regardless of our inattention or fault, is doing. Even more, we forget that God has promised to remain with us all days unto the end of time. We shall not be overcome, because our God is infinitely resourceful and so loved the world that he gave his only Son (Jn 3: 16). The priest is the memory of the Church, lest we forget.

Jesus and Courtship

Dating on college campuses has changed in the past fifty years. Only since 1972 has Notre Dame been co-educational, and dating prior to that depended mainly on women from St. Mary's College. There was not much easy and frequent camaraderie among the sexes because of the separation of campuses. Now at Notre Dame women and men cross paths many times a day. Friendships are well distinguished from the going-steady commitment that dating tended to generate rather quickly. A more uninhibited sexuality, for better of for worse, brings more intimacy without necessarily heading for the altar. Masturbation among young men is ever with us, and more commonly, I am told, with young women. Internet pornography is an epidemic that brings sadness at any time of night or day. The eternal courtship dance of the sexes goes on as ever, and its anxieties continue as well. College-age men and women know more about sex and remain more comfortable about what rarely was talked about before, but they seem as naïve and lost about love and romance as generations before. We experience true love only by a quite unpredictable grace. The complaint at Notre Dame continues to be that men and women find it hard to be at ease is an easy friendship with one another. They share classes, activities, and dining facilities every day, but side by side is often not a close association. Co-ed dorms seem the promised land, butNotre Dame remains a hold-out for single-sex residence halls. Maybe being together night and day would bond men and women, and one prescinds from issues of morality, nuisance, modesty, jealousies, and what have you in such imagined constant and familial companionship of the sexes. One wants at this time neither the quick courtship leading to romance and marriage, nor a hooking-up that leads to disappointment and often low self-esteem for not holding oneself more dear. What to do?

ONE COULD ARGUE that for a man a lovely young woman is the most beautiful vision he can hope to see, and for a woman her first-born newborn child is the most beautiful vision she can hope to see. That insight might explain how Mary managed so well her life with Jesus from Bethlehem to Calvary. She had found the pearl of great price. She beheld in her arms the most beautiful child of all time, and he was flesh of her flesh. What about Jesus? How did he appreciate the beauty of womankind in his life? How did Jesus negotiate the dance of courtship that preoccupies young men who seek their bride, and young women who also await the life-mate and father to be of their child?

How did Jesus thread his way through the many women who followed him and no doubt came to love him? Surely they fell in love with him. His qualities must have been ravishing from a human point of view. How did Jesus achieve friendship without courtship and without crossing boundaries expected of an honest man. Most men and women go a-courting, whether they are very aware of it or not. Not exactly on the make, they are tentative about a deep-seated question: is this one the one? Here is what I think. Jesus did not give signals that he was consciously or unconsciously courting women for any reason connected with their gender. Jesus treated all women with a respect that gave them the awareness they were loved for the person they were, whether sinner or saint, and that Jesus was not in the courting business. Women did not pick up the green and red lights that men simultaneously send out in our dating games. Women are good at picking up signals of incipient courtship and sexual desire. Pure friendship without implicit courtship must have been a hallmark of Jesus. The women who followed Jesus knew he was not hitting on them, and they loved him all the more. He just loved them and they knew it. That simple "pure of heart" trumps all. Not disinterested, but not flirting, he cared for a friend and he knew her as a woman. In him there was only light, warm and clear, a love that had no calculation, no hesitation, and no unconscious agenda.

Did Jesus Marry?

Marriages at Notre Dame come along in season and out with a weekend regularity. Adolescent males, and sometimes females, pursue the Internet for sexual titillation. Easing an addiction may describe the plight of many young people with so much sexual energy in their youth. Gay relationships meet with less resistance in our students than in their parents and mentors. They will attend the wedding of their friends, and bring them to their own weddings. There is not much said about the vocation to a single life. It may not be seen even as an option. The celibate religious life for men or for women attracts a few Notre Dame students, but celibacy by and large seems an obstacle, among obstacles, to a happy life. Less than perfect role models of any and all sexual choices but confuses the picture, the deliberation, and the discernment. So, why did Jesus not marry?

THE GOSPELS are not pure history. The account of the life of Jesus gives us an historical theology or a theological history, wherein the eyes of faith and the video-camera of fact without fiction are blended. There is no evidence in the Gospels that Jesus married. Neither

207

wife or children appear on the scene. The recorded visit of Jesus to Nazareth does not include a family that he began. We do not know much of anything of the first thirty years of Jesus' hidden life in Nazareth. He may have married. Why not? And that may be a question to be thought through. He may have married and his wife died in childbirth of their first-born. In yet another way the cross may have crossed his life unknown to us. There is reason to doubt, however, that Jesus ever married, and reasons even more obvious to doubt that he undertook a secret marriage with Mary Magdalene, as fiction would have it. That the evangelists and early Christians covered up such a marriage is yet more of a stretch. That Mary Magdalene may have been a temptation of Jesus may have some traction, but not a seduction. Even the devil did not manage that.

So, why did Jesus not marry? In the Gospels, he obviously liked women, and women liked him. Jesus was a giver and not a taker. A wife, a home, a family of children would have been loved by Jesus. To them he would have given time, energy, and affection in all the ways a spouse and young children deserve and rightly claim of their man and their father. Jesus stayed briefly in each village in his travels, and he was driven to move ever on with his gospel message of the coming here and now of the Kingdom of God. So many to touch, so much to do, so little time, so few moments of grace and miracle. His heart was too big, his desires too comprehensive, his urgency too demanding for what marriage and family would entail were he both sensitive and responsive to its continual needs. Jesus tried to love everyone, and by so doing he risked the satisfaction of his own need for a particular intimacy. When he took Peter, James, and John to Mount Tabor in order to pray all night about the wisdom of going up to Jerusalem, where almost surely he would die, they fell asleep. In the Garden of Gethsemani, when his hour had come and he saw the crucifixion up close, they fell asleep again. None of them were at the foot of the cross. Only the women were there and at a distance, a sure sign they loved him and that they knew he loved them more than a marriage in this life could say or a body wed.

Gay: Fine by Me: Wait a Minute

Notre Dame claims to be an equal opportunity employer. Most universities in the United States claim as much. We do not discriminate on the basis of gender, religion, ethnic background, race, and age. That we do not discriminate on the basis of sexual orientation has not been included in so many words. Advocates insist that gays must be included explicitly or surely they will be excluded in some way. A Catholic university struggles with allegiance to Church teaching, which claims that gay persons must have equal rights, but that gay lifestyle in its sexual dimensions is disordered and immoral.

Whether latent prejudice or prudent foresight, Notre Dame has not included sexual orientation in its self-description of freedom to seek employment at the university. The student body is divided on this issue. A majority, I believe, support gay students, whom they know and count among their friends. A minority continues with verbal slurs, in private if not in public. Gays do not feel overwhelmingly welcome anywhere, and by and large not very welcome at Notre Dame. They may be loved, or told they will be loved, but they remain an "issue" at Notre Dame, and no one can get past the ambiguity. Love the sinner but hate the sin flies better on paper than in person. No doubt I oversimplify. Gay Catholics surely reveal a variety of experiences.

I AM NOT LOOKING for a fight on this issue; I do not even want to be controversial. I know the Church position on homosexuality, and I know there can be changes in that position, though how extensive any change may not be known by anyone. The acceptance of slavery in the world certainly suffered a setback in recent times. The acceptance of religious freedom certainly enjoyed an acceptance in recent times. Neither the State nor the Church has said its last word about homosexuality, whether in biology, behavior, morals, or lifetime relationships. I do not predict a radical change nor rule it out. I can hardly believe that Jews were so hated for centuries, or witches burned in New England, or heretics tortured to renounce their errors. War crimes and pedophilia continue to appall me, even as I know, but for the grace of God there go I. I do not pretend of myself to be better than anyone else. I do believe that some day we will apologize to gay people much as we have imperfectly done to Native Americans and Afro-Americans. We did not know them; we did not always love them. We found that meanness and cruelty were not beyond us. We meant well by and large, but we find that is never enough. Those who love a son or daughter, "come out" as gay or lesbian and perhaps headed for a lifetime commitment to someone in the hope of not living alone to the end of their days, know something the rest of us may yet need to learn.

Gay and lesbian people are not bad people, and it is not good for man or for woman to be alone. Gay sub-culture may disturb many of us, but hetero-sexual sub-culture has no cause to boast it is so much better. Sin abounds in all of us, of course, but we also believe where sin abounded, grace abounded the more.

CHAPTER SEVEN

PONDERINGS

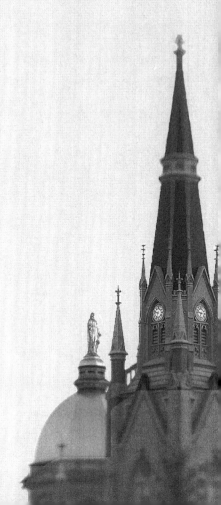

Lost Dreams Revisited

Human life might be described as our many goodbyes. Sooner or later we must say goodbye to most everyone we have known. We say goodbye to classmates as we graduate, to family when we leave home, indeed, to this world itself when we come to die. Just as all things in this life break, so too to all people in our lives in this world are parted from us. We also say our goodbyes to lost dreams, lost loves, lost friends, lost choices. We have lost alums at Notre Dame, whom we cannot trace nor find. Betrayals by State or Church, by home or school, broken promises and cruel words can all lead to losing and being lost. Alumni reunions have some success, but we often find them occasions to share our losses with others in the same boat. Springtime flowers and flowering trees at Notre Dame seem perfect and unspoiled, when leaves are fresh, green, clean, and without bug attacks. Then there is a long hot summer, and we know lost innocence in that recurrent heat, even as we do believe we will all meet again in the resurrection of the body and life everlasting.

215

THERE COMES A MOMENT somewhere in the middle of everyone's life when it becomes clear that our dreams will not all come true. It is either too late for us, or our ideals turned out too big for us. Either way, we know in our bones that our dreams will be unfulfilled. Human life is a broken one, an unfinished symphony, no matter how well the first notes harmonized. We have no lasting city. We have no control over other people, events, or most circumstances. We may have written the play we would direct, but the actors took over, and what appeared on the events stage is not what we had hoped. Though not what we had dreamed and planned. what happens in our life may prove in God's providence to be surprisingly hopeful.

There is a story in the Gospel about the journey of Jesus to the home of Jairus, an official whose daughter lay critically ill. Nothing happens along the way as planned. Jesus, on his way to do good, is interrupted by a woman in the crowd pressing around him. She merely touches the hem of his garment with hope that her bleeding, from which she suffered through twelve years of exhausted savings and unsuccessful doctoring, would at last be healed by Jesus, the man of God. And so it was. Jesus then tells her that her faith has made her whole. Jesus then goes to the daughter of Jairus, but he arrives too late. She has died. With great tenderness, Jesus takes her hand and wakes her from sleeping with the dead.

What is the moral of this Gospel story? When one suffers interruption it may be more important than our own plans. We are given our lines in the play of life by

God. Our own script is not workable. God's plans and God's dreams include our own dreams, if we allow God to dream in us. No problem known, however old and hopeless, is beyond God's mercy. The older woman, who is bleeding, is healed just when all her resources seemed exhausted. Jesus was interruptible; Jesus was available; Jesus is always available. The younger woman, the un-named daughter of Jairus, represents our lost inno-cence and unfulfilled dreams. We thought all that we had hoped for and all that we were given had died. We blame ourselves and cover our shame with despondent hopelessness. And yet, Jesus tells the child's family that she is not dead; she is only sleeping. Our innocence and our dreams, our youth and our hopeful childlike trust in God are not dead and gone. They are asleep, and even now in our tears, Jesus comes to waken us and those best parts in us of our lives when we dared to dream and to become like little children. To such as these there re-mains always the Kingdom of God, and unless we be-come like little children we shall not enter into its life. We are people with hope to bring.

Old Age Revisited

How a society treats the very young and the very old determines its values. Those who are vulnerable depend on those who are strong, and we declare our values in the treatment of those who cannot take care of themselves. Walking the walk is more important than talking the talk. Watch the parking lot etiquette after Sunday Church prayers. Check out the believer in God who goes home and kicks the dog. "Don't tell me; show me" remains always good advice. Human beings are living longer. Will we promote their living well? My mother lived to be ninety-seven, and when I retired from the faculty at Notre Dame, I was seventy years old. If I live to ninety-seven years, I have more years ahead of me in retirement than the twenty-five years I taught at Notre Dame. Our young students think they will never die. I believe that explains why they risk their lives so recklessly. But they surely will know old age. We have watched Pope John Paul II age gracefully, and on the campus of Notre Dame we watch President Emeritus Theodore Hesburgh, C.S.C. age gracefully. In my book they are both saints, both "Greats," who gave their lives unto their last breath in their old age to the people they guarded and led to green pastures as the good shepherd his sheep.

218

WHO WANTS TO LIVE FOREVER? In this world I would not think endless life a blessing, but more like a tragic destiny, much like that of Sisyphus, who rolled the rock to the rim of the mountain top only to have it escape his grasp and roll back down the hill, where he was condemned to push again against a ruthless gravity. To live forever here below is to go around in circles, like the earth around the sun, getting nowhere. Perhaps such a life would be vastly interesting for even millennia, but in the end, forever in this world would be boring. There is nothing new under the sun eventually, and "vanity of vanities all is vanity," as *Ecclesiastes* tells us (1: 2). Moreover, even the sun will burn out in time. Old age and approaching death from this perspective is a blessing. Eternal life with God is a promise that takes us out of this world to God who made this world, not as our true home or a lasting city, but as a passageway to the heart of God, which does not go around in circles getting nowhere, but cascades in wisdom and in joy for which all else we have ever known is but preparation. In our creator is our hidden name. In our savior, Jesus Christ the Lord, is our secret love life. In the Holy Spirit is the unimaginable life of God to which, after this our old age, we are enjoined forever.

And so, shall we say we do not want to live forever in this world? Shall we further say we want to die, and not maybe so, but surely so? And yet, this world is so lovely at times and so beautiful in places, that life seem indescribably precious on this earth. Even God could not bear to miss its enchantment in the flesh. Who does not at times prefer Christmas to Easter? Who does not prefer beginnings to endings, youth in its springtime to age in its autumn? We want to live, now and to come, in this life and in the life to come. I also want to die to this life, but not now. I am willing, but I am not inclined to volunteer.

And so, if this life is a walk with God in space and time, let us do it spritely. Let God lead, and the walk would be tuned right as God chooses. God is our companion on the journey, and Jesus, incarnate in the Christmas mystery of his birth in the stable, is forever enfleshed in our world. He remains really present with us in the bread we break with him on the way to our heavenly home. He came to bring us along with him back to where we began, conceived from the beginning in the great love of the Father Almighty – infinite, not in all possibilities, but in all actualities.

The Meaning of
Life Discovered in Old Age

Job interviews during senior year on any college campus loom large in the challenges of higher education. Rehearsals are rehearsed. Advice is sought. Neckties are knotted just so. A student asked me during my necktie-teaching years at Notre Dame how I tied such an attractive knot. Sadly I revealed it was but a clip-on tie. Women ponder scarves for color and draping, and their dress code may well surpass anything I am imagining. My advice to edgy students is simple. Tell them where you have been in your personal and educational life, where you think you stand now, and where you want to go and hope to go in the future. In short, give an account of your education and vocational dreams from past years to the present and on to the desired but unknown future. Why did you go to college? Why did you come to Notre Dame, or wherever you chose or God's providence led you? What purpose do you serve? What purpose in your life does Notre Dame serve?

THESE QUESTIONS COME to me late in my life. I find them easier to answer now than to entangle the mixed motives that brought me to Notre Dame as a freshman in the autumn of 1951. For starters, the University of Notre Dame was founded to give an education of quality with a Catholic perspective and a Catholic formation of character in so far as possible by classroom study, residential campus living, and sacramental life abundantly offered. Notre Dame cannot admit everyone, and so it chooses those who might be leaders in society and in the professions. Their impact on the common good would be greatest, because of their Notre Dame education and their subsequent life-vocation. When women moved into societal leadership in the same ways as men, Notre Dame changed from an all-male student body in order precisely to stay the same. Had it not changed in 1972, it would have changed its purpose from the education of future leaders in all areas of society to education of only men leaders.

Notre Dame knows its purpose and the meaning of its life. When I came to Notre Dame I had to learn my purpose. I came for many reasons, mixed motives, half-conscious reasons. I wanted to follow others I knew, to take the next step expected of me, You can fill in your own purposes and motives, complex and inarticulate as were mine. What I have learned over time with my Notre Dame education is just this. We find better reasons to continue our education than we had to begin it. In every vocation as well, whether marriage, religion, or career, we must find better reasons to stay on than one had to begin. We discover our purpose and the meaning of our life as we live along with the help of God's grace.

The old "Baltimore Catechism" told us succinctly of our purpose: "God made us to know him, to love him, and to serve him in this life and to be happy with him forever in the next." That is ultimately why we go to school, why we come to Notre Dame, why we get up out of bed every morning, why we labor, and why we love our family and our friends. We may not have meant it so when we were younger. We grow in recognition of our mission. Our purpose-driven life and our mission in life -- our vocation in life and our providential guidance in life -- turn out to be all of the same cloth. God made us also to know us, to love us, and to be happy with us in this life and forever in the next. It may take some education, and surely some time, to discover that God's purpose with us is our purpose with God.

Re-member

Times of spiritual retreat and times of alumni visitation are surely times of remembrance and even, one might say, poignant nostalgia. We both rejoice in the past when its glow brings gratitude, and we also mourn the inevitability of its passing. Archives of all kinds thrive at Notre Dame. We would live in the present moment but remain conscious at the same time of the past. We are good at multi-tasking, and especially so at a university. Students and faculty juggle many balls every day, and many of them are in the air simultaneously. When finally one can do only one thing at a time, it may well be the sign that it is time to stop our endless projects and to prize what has been and ever will be -- what God has done in us, with us, and through us

.

WHAT HAVE YOU that you have not received? Good question, and the answer is — not a thing. What lifetime can you hope to last forever? Most people might claim their life endures, or soul and body inseparably united in the hope of resurrection and eternal life perdure. But, what of this life's experience can you take with you? What do we have that no man can take from us? I want to answer that only our memories endure, and even these are fragile and vulnerable. The future moment is not yet, and the next second of my life on earth is not guaranteed to me, nor to you reading this book at this moment. The present moment flows by like an endless swift-flowing river. The moment is gone into the past and reaching into the un-guaranteed future with an alarming speed that seems only to increase with our age. What we can claim to have and to hold is only our memories of the past. Each night we forget them all in sleep, and we hope that we and they are all there in the morning. Each year we forget a bit more of them, and sometimes even all of them, as one slides into a kind of oblivion depicted in the many faces of dementia.

In the end our memories are safely kept forever only in God, who is treasure hunter and not garbage collector. God remembers us and our memories that we would keep. God re-members us in the resurrection of our body, and God re-members us when he says in what Jesus his son says: "Indeed I will remember you when I come into my kingdom. 'This day you will be with me in paradise' " (Lk 23: 43). This present moment, the past moments with all our memories, and life everlasting in the future will coalesce in God's re-membering. We will be secure in God's everlasting now, which binds together everything that is and was and is to come, to the glory of God, as it was in the beginning, is now, and will be forever, world without end. Amen.

Caretakers

One of the turning points in a college career comes when the student defends the campus because they feel at home -- not exactly ownership, but one belongs. It is now my campus, and I am more inclined to pick up trash on the grass than carelessly throw it there. I have become a caretaker of something I have come to care about and of which I intend now to be more care-full. Later in life such care turns into donations and volunteer service to an alma mater one has come to love. The trustees of the university are also its trusted caretakers. They are responsible as are owners, but they are entrusted with the care of the university and its mission, given to them as a "deed in trust" to continue Notre Dame as a Catholic institution of higher learning. So God gave planet earth to human beings with a "deed in trust," that they be loving and careful caretakers of the common good. The world is not mine, nor ours; it belongs to God. Holy Cross religious write in their books "Ad Usum " followed by their name, because the book is for their use not their arbitrary disposal. All of us should be non-profit servants and caretakers in this world, because all life is a gift of God we are given to care for.

FOR WHOM AND FOR WHAT am I responsible for? To whom and to what am I responsible? The word "responsible" should be pondered. "Able to respond" decodes "responsible." Willing to respond might seem an even more accurate definition. When Adam and Eve hid from God in the Garden, they were unwilling to respond to God's question: "Who told you that you were naked"? When Cain responded to God asking the whereabouts of Cain's brother, Abel, Cain did not truly respond. He was not responsible. "Am I my brother's keeper"? implied he was not. Our lives, however, must embody the opposite response. We are our brother's and our sister's keeper, and the only response to that question should be how are we to be responsible to and responsible for others before God. We cannot realistically be responsible for everyone and everything on planet earth. Compassion fatigue is a real syndrome. Our loyalty begins where charity begins – at home. We own our responsibilities to our parents and our elders, our schools and our mentors, our homeland in the various ways it may call upon us for support. We own our responsibilities for our children, the fruit of our bodies, and for the children of our mind and heart, birthed in the many endeavors of human creativity that gives life to others.

Regrets

College students seem to have ever-increasing choices about their work after graduation. Options before graduation to specialize also have increased. Everywhere in a modern university one is faced with the road not taken. One sees the same phenomenon in human relationships. One can marry only one person at a time, date only one person at a time if the dating is more than casual, and choosing one person over another reveals again the road not taken. Given the many roads and given the anxiety of commitment to one over another, it is no wonder that regrets haunt our lives. We may have chosen well, and the regrets are moderated, even if felt at times. We may have chosen poorly or events went badly, and now our regrets are persistent and sometimes bitter. If gratitude is the source of human happiness in the wanting of what one has, then regretful resentment is the source of human unhappiness in the demand of having what one wants.

WHAT ARE WE SUPPOSED to do with these mind-numbing, soul-crushing, clear memory moments full of regrets? What of the crashing recognition of what I could have done, should have done, would have done, if I only

knew then what I know now, and if only I was the person
back then that I think I am today. The saddest words
of men are these: it might have been. Now it is too late.
Now it cannot be; we cannot go back. We are eaten alive
by regrets. If only I could do it all over again. My de-
cisions would change; my appreciations would grow. To
which one is inclined to say — maybe yes and maybe no.
Life in our mind, tormented with guilt and regret, will
always be easier than real life on the ground. We may
have grown; we may be different, but mistakes, sins,
blind spots are with us always, today as well as yesterday,
and tomorrow as well. We remain fallible; we are sinful
even when we are graced. We are created good, and we
always have been and we always will be. What we need
to do is to forgive ourselves, our past and our present,
our friends and those friends we call enemies, because
we have never met them soul to soul. Human beings are
all the same in this. We are tangled lovers. We mean well
even when we do wrong. Hurt people hurt people. Ignorant people do ignorant things. Not well loved people do
not love others well. We are mightily sinning and we are
mightily sinned against. So, how do we forgive and relieve all these regrets ?

Short answer: trust in God and in God's love for
us all. Long answer: think through the implications of
God's creation of the world and our belief in God, the
Father-Almighty, creator of heaven and earth. If God
is infinite, and no finite god is worth the name, then
how can anything be something, since an infinite God
is by definition everything that is. How can anything

be created if God already fills all? How can God with-
draw that something or someone might be at all? How
can God, who is everything, create out of nothing? Why
anything? How anything? Creation is not logically possible, and creation from nothing makes logical sense as
the only way, but yet baffles the human mind and imagination. In the beginning we believe God created the
world out of nothing and that this vast cosmos is also
under the providence of the Father-Almighty, who in
realm of being is the divine creation and in the realm
of doing is the divine providence. We believe in the creation of a sovereign Creator and in the providence of a
sovereign Father-Almighty. We believe in the infinite
love that is infinite power and the infinite power that is
infinite love. The remedy for our regrets is to trust in
the God of our beginnings and the God of our endings.
In the ending, as in the beginning, God will create the
world and call it very good. If "in the beginning" God
creates from nothing, "in the ending" God will create
from everything – our failures, sins, regrets, mistakes,
tears, and tragedies as well as our joys and pro-cre-
ations, virtues, successes, and comedies. In the ending
God will create a new heaven and a new earth from everything, just as God created the heavens and the earth
from nothing in the beginning. In the ending no drop
will be wasted, no tear shed in vain, no sin left unfor-
given, no evil left unredeemed. God will write straight
with crooked lines. And to those who love God, it will
be revealed that all things commingle unto good in the
hands of the Creator of everything "in the beginning"

from nothing and "in the ending" from everything —
good and bad, affirmed and regretted. Mercy and truth
shall kiss. And "God will wipe away every tear" (Rv 7:
17), regrets and all.

What the Past Has Said

In your first year at Notre Dame, you do not choose your roommate. In our first days on planet earth, we did not choose our parents and their families. Grandparents and Godparents are given us. There may be an element of choice in marriage, but it was not the newborn's choice. Our life is a chance event from this world's perspective. Our parents' encounter in the first instance seems often to have been accidental. We are not accidental to God, however, we are intended by God from all eternity. We are most truly God's son or daughter, and but lent to our parents, who pro-create on behalf of God the creator of heaven and earth and of us all. It may take a village to raise a child, and it may take a university campus to educate a student. We take pride in our ancestry, event though we did not earn our place. We belong to our family and to our alma mater more than they belong to us. We all may be cousins in the original genetic lines of the human race, but we have even more than that in common and in debt. We are all made of dust, stardust to be precise. Every molecule of our body and our earth once was in a star, and we live even now by starlight that grows our food to sustain our life. Our ancestry is four-

teen billion years ago, and if time itself was given a be-
ginning by the infinite creator of all, then we are eternally
in the mind and heart of God, and that surely seems a
remarkable ancestry.

IN THE YEAR OF 2007 on September 11th, I happen to
have been writing of my grandfather, Henry Nicholas.
He fought in the Civil War for the South. He was cap-
tured at the Battle of Vicksburg toward the end of the
war. He was told to walk on back to the bayous of Louisiana where he came from. I never knew my maternal
grandfather. He died in the influenza epidemic in the
early twentieth century before I was born. He might easily have died in the Civil War, or undertaken a smaller
family. I might never have been, or should I say, I might
never have been me.

Some people think that slavery would have faded
away because of economic factors, even without a violent struggle, much less a long bloody war begun over
politics more than over emancipation. I try to draw a
parallel with the struggle to prevent abortion. To many
Americans abortion is murder, and most any civil dis-
obedience is justified to stop the holocaust of the helpless unborn. To many other Americans abortion is a
question of a woman's freedom to birth a child under
circumstances she can hope to manage. I cannot equate
abortion and murder in my mind, though I say unques-
tionably that abortion is wrong. Even were it the lesser
of two evils, it is evil. Would I have been a slave own-
er were I born a hundred years before my time? Proba-

bly so. Am I soft on abortion and hard on slavery, now that slavery has clearly passed away in its public manifestations. Probably so. And yet, what should we think of all the conceptions that nature aborts spontaneously, about which women have no control nor even awareness. If we believe in an after life, are all these conceived children who were never brought to term by nature's own selection, to be persons in the after life? And what of the miscarriage, whom the mother does know about and greatly cares about? And what if it were me? And what about my grandfather with bullets whizzing around his head? Are we not fragile, vulnerable, contingent, and providential from the womb to the tomb. And then, why me remains such a poignant question. My given name is Nicholas Richard. My grandfather was Henry Nicholas, and my grandmother was Aglae Richard. My mother was forty years old when I was born, and she was the last of thirteen children. And I am me, and my ancestry goes all the way back to the "big bang" when there was no astronomical space. "How me" seems the easier question. "Who me" and "why me" remains the true mystery of ancestry.

So Few So Much to So Many

College campuses now have emergency-call plans in the event of a gunman wreaking havoc on the campus. The Virginia Tech massacre was neither the first nor will it be the last. One troubling student in a residence hall can inconvenience everyone. One drunk can keep up half the dorm half the night, cleaning up and calming down. One malicious vandal can spoil the beauty and the serenity of the campus. One angry fan can tarnish the reputation of the whole school at an athletic event. One out-of-control fan can saddle an innocent basketball team with a technical foul. It has happened. And what of the well-meaning Notre Dame graduate who snatched the foul ball from the outfielder's glove and left the Chicago Cubs jinxed yet again? We believe in the Communion of Saints, that is, we believe that we all suffer from the sins of all and that we are all blessed by the virtues and graces of all. We are in the same boat together, for better or for worse, and our lives impact the lives of those with whom we live. Nowhere is this more evident than in families, and perhaps clearly so in campus residences, where so many live so closely together and where so few can do so much for good or bad to so many.

IN A WORLD OF SIX BILLION PEOPLE and counting it is hard to believe than any one person counts for much. Surely one may suppose that no one person can change the course of history. Perhaps a king of old or a prime minister of today can make a decision to go to war, and the impact can change the lives of millions, quite likely for the worse. That an unknown person with no authority can change the lives of everyone on Planet Earth seems nigh impossible. Granted, Thomas Edison's light bulb is almost everywhere, and Shakespeare, Mozart, Handel, and Tchaikovsky, to name a few individuals, have left indelible impressions on us all.

Who comes to mind for me, however, is someone like D.B. Cooper, whose high-jacking of a commercial airliner created inspection lines that reach around the world and have more recently culminated in shoeless passengers passing between beefed-up metal detectors. I think as well of someone like Mohammad Atta, whose terrorism provoked the only super-power in the world of his day to pour billions of dollars and millions of lives into war against attack in an uncertain future.

In the Bible, the sin of Adam and Eve began a sinful world, which human history inherits and which burdens all human beings. Our ancestors were both sinning and sinned against. When Abraham bargained with God to spare the city if only ten good men were found, he hoped to keep striking the bargain until his point was made (Gn 18: 32). Suppose only one good man is found, would that be enough to save us all?

Does love spread like violence spreads, I want to ask?

Could one person's love touch the whole world? Are we so linked as human beings that all of us impact all of us however imperceptibly? Do we pass it on, good or bad, no matter how or what. Does a Mother Teresa inspire around the world. Does the redemptive love of Jesus Christ intermingle in the lives of the living and the dead, the past and the future? Does the shadow of the cross fall upon all human beings, and the light of the resurrection give hope around the globe to everyone, whether or not they see light or know only darkness? Are we one body, one world, one people, caught up in the same story and the same conflict of good and evil together with the triumph of God's love in us? The Communion of Saints is a most optimistic belief of Christians, because not only are we all in it together, but God-with-us has joined us in the flesh and in our history in irrevocable and unsurpassable love.

Hidden Violence

College-age students take risks with their lives. It goes with the territory. They think they are immortal, and that nothing bad can happen to someone who feels so strong and healthy. They can outfight or outrun their dangers, should being born under a lucky star prove not enough. That children grow up at all, and continue to live as well, seems to me much a miracle. Near misses seem a happy part of the teen-agers' repertoire of horror stories, stories told to their parents thirty years later and to their friends thirty minutes later. Automobile disasters are a matter of split seconds and, believe it or not, most drivers learn distractedly on the job and live to tell about it. Such young lives are about enough to make one believe in divine providence. God might just have plans for young women and men that the Almighty has invested in, and what God wants, God gets. Our culture continues to shape ever more violent movies and computer games, and we play them, trusting that such violence is make-believe. That we have become callous from over-exposure remains the question that haunts me.

WE ARE INDEED SHOCKED when three thousand people die suddenly in the terrorist attack on the World Trade Center in New York. We lament the casualties of the long war being fought in Iraq at the time I am writing. Yet we kill thousands a month on our highways in this country alone, let alone around the world, and we injure and maim some hundred thousand and more a year, year after year, in this our country. Why are we not more outraged with the killing fields of the automobile than the far less destructive terrorist attacks around the world. Perhaps the world of the automobile is an economic and necessary evil, and the world of terrorism a wasteful and gratuitous evil. AIDS infects millions, but malaria year after year outscores all epidemics by far. Include malnutrition and unclean drinking water, and the enormous scourges of our humanity seem to be the ones we routinely overlook, having become accustomed to the slaughter the way it is. We cannot imagine what to do about issues so vast, so complex, so beyond a simple solution of any kind. And we do enjoy selective perception, seeing what we choose to see, weighing what seems important to us, spinning the world according to news media that need stories of violence that are new (news) and that renew alarm, which keeps one tuned and allows people to make a living of those making a killing. No one to blame comes to mind. We are all caught up in the web. We mean well. We can hardly bear to look always at this cauldron of human violence. Indeed, we truly suffer compassion fatigue. And yet of such violence I have to write, because at times it seems the only alternative to futile tears.

Dorms For The Dead

Death and dying seem totally incongruous on a campus of young men and women in their prime. Youth reigns; life flourishes in college years. And yet, some students die every year, more likely from freak car accidents and unexpected and unexplained cancers. Funerals or memorial masses at Notre Dame for our fallen students are well attended and the Basilica is full of mourners. The whole campus saddens. When the elderly are buried here, whether from the faculty or from the parish, the attendance is reduced. If you live long enough, you will outlive your contemporaries. Someone has to be last, alas, just as someone among the students has to be first. "God, Country, and Notre Dame" is carved over the eastern door of the Basilica at Notre Dame. It is a memorial to World War I, and the Peace Fountain where the old Basketball Arena once stood, gathers up the subsequent wars of our country. Many of our Notre Dame graduates gave up their lives for their country. I am sure students are mildly aware of their mortality, and their nickname for the new columbaria constructed in the Cedar Grove Cemetery at the head of Notre Dame Avenue says much of that awareness. "Dorms for the Dead" may simply re-

240

fer to these resting places for the cremains of the Notre Dame family, but the succinct phrase echoes an awareness that all dormitories implicitly speak of a long sleep.

IT IS EARLY MORNING IN OCTOBER. Hot coffee cup in hand, I walk up the narrow path from the back of Corby Hall to the front sidewalk. Grotto traffic plies this narrow and twisty path scarcely wide enough to pass someone coming the other way. This morning it is foggy and dark at this hour. I whistle a tune for fear of surprising a raccoon near the dumpster, or worse, a skunk. I have seen skunks at night in front of the Main Building, make of that what you will. No animal was around the path as usual this morning, and I wondered where they were at this moment. And where do all the bunnies, squirrels, mice, coons, skunks, and varmints go to die. Have you ever seen a mammal cemetery for four-legged critters? Do they bury themselves? Do they head off campus to die? Do they die lingering deaths under the bushes out of sight and leaving no smell of death and decay? I wonder.

Human dying is more complicated. I try to make death simple. Three things the dying must do come to mind. Ask your family and friends to forgive you; thank them for all they are to you and have given to you; tell them you love them – then you are done. In letters of condolence I make the same few points to everyone I know no matter the details. My remarks are obvious, but I say them. No one can take his or her place in one's life. A conversation never finished must now be postponed.

One's own mortality moves uncomfortably closer when death claims someone we loved. And finally, we are people with hope in God, with hope to bring to any dire predicament — and then you are done.

My Own Death

I am not sure what others have thought of their death during their college years. I cannot remember thinking of it at all. Risks that look so foolish now would never have been taken were I thinking I might actually die. Awareness of how precious every day truly is would have been in the ascendancy, and I would not have neglected so many beautiful things and persons in my life, in assuming they would always be given me. In short, young people by and large are oblivious of the poignancy of life in its fragile goodness and its ultimate and omnipresent vulnerability. In the Odyssey, a book read by me only when I was a professor in the Great Books Program at Notre Dame, there is an episode that describes Odysseus enchanted and enthralled by a beautiful goddess on a wonderful island of delight with the promise that he need never die with her at his side. In a short time he tires of bliss, and he yearns to be on his way to his home and his wife, where he will find suitors wooing her and plotting to kill him. Only when we recognize the jeopardy and finite contingent quality of human life do we come to cherish every moment as irreplaceable and precious beyond calculation, or even imagination.

WHEN I WAS YOUNGER, I was braver. I was not afraid to die. My faith was strong and my health even stronger. Vibrant vitality gives courage as nothing else. Now I am older. Now I am old. Now I feel weak around the knees and not so strong at heart. My faith may be in its twilight, not the dark night of the soul the saints endured, but a dusk not nearly so comfortable as yesteryear. I say it to myself for the first time. I am afraid to die. Of course, I would have admitted that sooner in a gesture of humility, but at the core I did not believe I was afraid to die. Now I say it. I am afraid to die, really afraid to die. Moreover, I am afraid of being afraid to die, and I am afraid of being afraid of being afraid to die. Suddenly there is an endless regress and the ground of my self-confidence seems like a challenge to walk on water. I think of a Woody Allen quip: "I am not afraid to die; I just don't want to be there when it happens."

My prayer life has become my night life, and my night life, spent recovering from the day's demands in a comfortable but lonely bed, has become my prayer life. If I am awake in bed, as often I am, it is dark and death is not un-thought of. Is not sleep a rehearsal for that opening night? I am afraid I will not know my lines, and even if I did, I might forget them. I am afraid to die, and I admit how easy it has become to pray. There is no other resource left in me to cling to. Of course, I can still parse my theology, but I expect to forget that too, and perhaps sooner than I think. Memory is no resource with a guarantee. And so I pray. I pray I will not forget how to pray. I continue to be afraid of being afraid, just as worry about losing sleep loses sleep. Perhaps I am just too anxious. "Who is Afraid of Virginia Woolf"? Well, I am. And "Do not go gentle into that dark night" may be good advice, but I wonder if a protest or a fight would do any good. I may have lost my memory, and no doubt my courage, but I have not lost my mind – yet. And so I pray. And I prefer Jesus to the poets. "My God, my God, why have you forsaken me" needs always to be balanced with what I hope never to forget: "Father, into your hands I commend my spirit."

Yes or No

Halloween has become a major festival in America. Paraphernalia of all kinds can be bought. Costumes of all kinds can be rented. Parties for the college generation, and outfits for a supervised evening stroll for the youngsters now takes time and costs money. Notre Dame celebrates Halloween with or without disguises. It's always a good time to drink in college years, and it does not take much of an excuse to postpone studies and take a night off. Scary movies and thematic décor inside and outside the residence hall adds to the glamour of the evening. A mild awareness of the eve of all-hallows, that is, all-saints does hover. Graveyard humor is not much analyzed, but the following day does bring heaven to mind, and the day after, All Souls Day, something more dreadful. When the saints go marching in is played against the lingering memory that sometime ago there was something to dread and fear about one's last day. What was that all about might well be the campus question today.

Every story has an ending. Every life has an ending in this world. How blessed we would be on our death bed, should we speak of our hope in life everlasting to those who were companions of our lives. How we die may be the best gift we can give to the living, when we must leave those we love. Judgment comes to mind when faith in God encounters death. Shall we meet the God of mercy or the God of justice, and how can God be both at once? We fear bench-justice in the great judicial session in the sky.

Some people imagine judgment will be only a revelation. We will see ourselves in the truth of our lives, and God, who knows all, need say nothing. We will judge ourselves. Other people imagine judgment will be only a fulfillment. When the Bible ends with the Christian scriptures last words, "Come, Lord Jesus," Christians were not in fear and dread of judgment. They were not thinking of an awful final coming of Jesus. "Come, Lord Jesus" is not about anticipation of a final exam, but rather it is about the long-awaited commencement exercise that begins a new life in eternal life. Our God is a treasure hunter and not a garbage collector, and while it is true we can hide from God, we cannot outrun God's love for us. Judgment will be a revelation not so much of our many sins, but of God's many graces. Judgment will be the "it is finished" of the consummate artist who steps back to admire the finished masterpiece. Judgment will sound more like the love story of Jesus who took our sins on himself and gave us his last breath to say to us, "it is finished" (Jn 19:30). All is fulfilled. Redemption and salvation will be revealed as God's providential and mysterious care of us all.

What about hell? That is a problem, and one should

248 / THE HEART OF NOTRE DAME

never pull the teeth of the Gospel. What about unre-
pentant sinners? Let us say first of all that God has no
desire that we fail to accept his love for us. In God's
courtship of our assent to God's love, God is infinitely resourceful. It seems almost arrogant and surely presumptuous on our part to assume we can outrun God. I
also recognize the necessity to say that if one can freely say "yes" to God, one must be able freely to say "no"
to God. Milton's Satan's boast: "better to reign in hell
than to serve in heaven" is served up with much poetic
license. Such a choice is absurd, even if absurd is possible. The Church does not claim it knows who is in hell,
pace Dante's "Inferno," nor that this or that villain is
surely in hell, nor that anyone at all is in hell or will
ever be in hell. We do not know how God's justice and
God's mercy do kiss. The Church defends only human
freedom to say "no," and she counts always on God's
grace. Of the rest of the story we know nothing. Hell is
not a place with space and time coordinates. Hell is not
God's torture chamber, for even we, too often cruel human beings, know human torture is abominable. God
surely is infinitely better than we. Fire and brimstone
are more poetry than theology. Hell remains separation
from God, and to be separated from everything and everyone is hell enough. We can hope, nonetheless, that no
one manages to refuse God's infinitely resourceful grace
that is God's love in our lives. — and to do so for a lifetime knowingly and hopelessly.

The Last Day

During college years one can hardly imagine that there will be a last day on campus. Graduation can be imagined, but that silently and inevitably there will be a last day to walk the campus seems harder to comprehend. So many days are guaranteed to intervene. There is no hurry. The last day is far away. And then one day the last day is today. Where did the time go? When did we become old? Do all good things end? What will be left from the ravages of time? What of life after Notre Dame, and more profoundly, what of life after Planet Earth? What will the future be?

"FEAR OF THE LORD" is one of the counsels of the Bible. We are to be reverent in the calling upon God. We are not to be presumptuous that mercy and God's love could be used as a license to get away with murder. Sins are forgiven; sins are not swept under the rug. God is infinitely compassionate, but we need to remember God is neither blind nor our punching bag for self-indulgence. The more elderly among us may have learned fear of the Lord from "hell and brimstone" sermons, now no longer in vogue. And yet, we must never make God in our image. We rule each other in part by threat and consequences. God's rule is much more subtle and infinitely sovereign. What God wants to do, God does, in ways that are not our ways. God persuades, but with a persuasion that is internal to our mind and heart, gentle but effective, as befits the grace of God, who is both provident and creative. God holds human freedom without compromise, yet holds all of us in the palm of his hand.

In the Genesis account of creation, God creates humankind on the sixth day, and on the seventh day God rested. Suppose the sixth day is a very long day and the creation of human beings never quite finished in this world until the last day. Only then God rests and creation is complete. We are told by St. Paul that we cannot imagine heaven. "Eye has not seen, nor ear heard, nor has it entered into the mind of man, what God has prepared for those who love him" (I Cor 2:9).

Each one of us remains a center of the universe, not the center. We can comprehend it all in so far as our mind might possibly be capable of being raised by God's grace to see God face to face. We are not the center of the universe, or the center of all that is. We are neither the creator nor the pantocrator, nor the infinite mystery of God that contains all being and is not contained by it. Only God is unique. Only God knows the view from everywhere. Only looking through God's eyes of glory will we ever see, as creatures enabled by God's gratuitous love to see the view from everywhere. I think of heaven and the last day as an infinite kaleidoscope of all views of reality and all simultaneous and forever and endlessly "the love that moves the sun and stars." That love is the love in the ending as it was in the beginning. No wonder we proclaim: "Glory to the Father, and to the Son, and to the Holy Spirit, as it was in beginning, is now, and will be forever."

What the Future Will Say

What will Notre Dame look like fifty years from today? What did we learn from the past and what will we learn from the future? Good judgment is learned from the experience of bad judgments. To be wise is to have changed one's mind, and to be truly wise is to have changed one's mind often. In our moments of nostalgia and perhaps in times of a class reunion we may be prompted to review our own past with its joys and sorrows, good calls and bad calls. No one learned to walk without falling, and no one learned to grow up without embarrassment. We may wonder what people will finally say of us at our funeral ceremonies. Speak no evil of the dead is a good rule of thumb, but often at funerals one hears of the goodness of a person never quite told to that person in person. We are not judges of ourselves or of our university. Time will tell, or better yet, God will tell, and that with both wisdom and mercy.

WHAT WILL BE SAID of our era in the future? How will historians treat our conduct – what we thought we knew and what we chose to do? We look back on medical practice of past decades and find pitiable blunders. For

252

centuries doctors did not know of germ transmission and septic precautions. Blood-letting was a fine theory, but it weakened patients rather than healing them. What will they say of our practices decades in the future? Will our drug-experimental treatments of a myriad of mental distresses seem primitive and misguided? Will our treatment of homosexuals be found benighted? One wonders. Should we pause and let the cold water of future generations now wash over what might be our contemporary hubris? Every generation thought it knew more than the past and did not think much of how it would also be surpassed by a future that would itself be surpassed. Truth comes hard, but maybe we can learn from past mistakes.

My mother lived almost one hundred years, and she began her life with oil lamps and the horse and buggy. She lived to see electric grids and men on the moon. Will there be an Edison light bulb to rescue our energy-gluttonous carbon consumption? Will technology, perhaps now even unimagined, once more save us from dwindling resources and environmental consequences? One wonders.

We find it hard to believe that we rounded up or led to death one way or the other the entire native population of North America. We find it hard to believe that our genteel and loving Christian families of the Slave States could not imagine what was so wrong about slavery. We cannot imagine how Germany that gave us cutting-edge science and technology as well as Bach, Beethoven, Brahms, Mahler, Schumann, Schubert, and Wagner could have played on as Jews en masse were burned.

I have lived within the ambience of the University of Notre Dame for one-third or more of its history. What of the next fifty years? Will Notre Dame be the university I now know? What of the United States of America in the world a half-century in the future? And what of the Catholic Church, that can and cannot change, that has wobbled and perdured through centuries that both blessed its existence and near blighted it for good? One wonders. Only God knows, the God who is the Father of mercies, whose providence is sovereign. Thank God.

The Bricks

IF YOU LOOK OVER the whole campus of Notre Dame from the upper windows of the library, the buildings are so numerous and diverse that the whole university seems a wonderland, an incredible accomplishment of private initiative and labors of love united in a shared vision of a city of intellectual and spiritual excellence in education. It is a bit of a trick to prize proudly both the amplitude and affluence of Notre Dame in its bricks and to recognize that the glory of this world is passing and that all the buildings will eventually be abandoned, because we have here no lasting city and no tower of Babel as well. Wisdom and communion with God flourish here by the grace of God alone, though the buildings are to the university as our body is to our soul. We are, of course, not just our body, but we cannot think nor pray without it. We could manage with fewer bricks, and we could well be detached from this beautiful campus. However, as Thomas Merton remarked, one cannot be detached until one is attached. One cannot pass beyond the visible Notre Dame until one has passed on foot within its walls.

I look at the University of Notre Dame. It remains

a magnificent creation of voluntary belief in a vision of education with quality and with soul. Who would have dreamed such a city could be built, a new Atlantis from the woods and fields of pioneer Indiana. And yet, I see its fragility, and I know its bricks are not the kind of rock the psalmist had in mind when he sang: "The Lord is my rock and my salvation" (Ps 18: 2). In astronomical perspective we are but a speck of sand upon a speck of a planet in a speck of solar system in a speck of a galaxy among billions of galaxies with billions of stars. Maybe some day we will no longer need these bricks, the old yellow ones, which those who most love the place love, and the new modern brick that ties together more or less the eclectic architecture of the campus, more like a patchwork quilt than a garment woven of whole cloth. Maybe some day the college will be an entirely electronic world, linking by voice and picture thousands of people in ample interactive enrichment today even unimaginable. Maybe. But I wonder what will compare to the Notre Dame shadows in the moonlight, the large spaces enclosed by the bricks, the mates we know in the flesh, the angels we can almost touch, the circus come to our town and one that is not virtual. I place my wager on the bricks that were blessed at their foundation.

The buildings of Notre Dame form an architectural garden. Mid-century cinder-block stands alongside of neo-gothic and most everything in between. There is a harmony in the color of the bricks and a diversity in the many designs, which with their gables and gargoyles, nooks and crannies, are related to one another by an architectural vision that changed hands many times over the decades. Even St. Peter's Basilica exhibits the mixed metaphor stemming from Rubens, the original architect, from Michelangelo who prevailed in the design of the dome, and Bernini, who finished the final construction. A university is very much a work in progress, and it is no exaggeration to call Notre Dame a perpetual construction site. I often pray that Notre Dame does not overbuild. Donor buildings and hero buildings are sometimes temptations to expand. Bigness may not be bad, but such gain may create a condition that the left hand no longer know what the right hand is doing. Bureaucracy and constantly rising fixed costs weigh down campuses as well as empires. Every new building requires maintenance, cleaning, insurance, heating and cooling, grounds work, renewal, utilities, and sewerage. The campus forever seems to display either a new building or a down to the bone renovation of an old one. The cleanliness and good maintenance of the more than one hundred building at Notre Dame is something to boast about. But the Gospel warning still stands: "What does it profit a man to gain the whole world and suffer the loss of his soul" (Mk 8: 36) and "Thou fool, this night thy life will be required of thee" (Lk 12: 20).

Their blood is in the bricks, so it is said. Blood, sweat, and tears are more easily imagined in the early days of Notre Dame. The Brothers of Holy Cross mined the clay at the bottom of the lake and formed and fired the distinctive yellow bricks by the thousands that identify readily the oldest buildings at the center of the campus.

Without a front loader nor a gas-fired oven, they worked with horses and block and tackle to bring firewood and to pull clay from the bottom. It is easy to imagine the blood of everyone who labors at Notre Dame in the bricks.

If only the bricks could talk in classroom and dormitory, what stories they could tell of what they heard from class after class. Our buildings have served others faithfully and stood by to support the most important project in the world. Upon the education and formation of the next generation of youth depends all the generosity and wisdom that will be applied by whatever means to whatever problems of the future. The bricks and mortar have a sacredness because they are holy from years of faithful service in the highest course. They are what they are. They give of themselves without question. They possess nothing but themselves. They belong to others while being themselves. I am not sure I want to take the bricks for our model of sanctity, but they do arouse in us all a feeling of the "halls of wisdom."

On the porch of Corby Hall, once upon a time a student residence, the custom was for each student to pencil his name and graduation year on a single brick. Fifty or more years of students were on display until the bricks were, alas, power-washed in the Millennium clean-up. Notre Dame is made up of its people and not of its bricks, just as the Church is made up of living stones. The family of Notre Dame and the Communion of Saints share a resemblance. Buildings will erode to dust in time. Only people live forever. The blood of our students, faculty, friends, benefactors, and alums is in the bricks, even as our ultimate hopes are in heaven.

When monasteries grow too large, they divide and start a new foundation. Community life seems to be diminished when numbers are either too small or too large. St. John's College in Annapolis started a second campus in Santa Fe. Teaching and research universities, as Notre Dame wishes to be, require a certain amount of building facilities and specialized faculty. Notre Dame is a small city; the nation is a yet larger city; the Church would be the largest city of all, encompassing and including all of humanity past, present, and future. Bigness presents some problems and solves others. Small is beautiful, but so is big when transformed. Jesus came not to give us a new world, but to transform this world. Creation in all its many bricks is not the enemy to be overcome, bracketed, or destroyed. The world with both its complexity and affluence, its simplicity and poverty, is to be transfigured. It is a daring and bold vision of a new heaven and new earth, where the bricks are not unworthy, and mere dust is given life, and we, whose bodies are made of that same stardust as the bricks, are to live forever. Whatever the education and formation of young men and women in the city of Notre Dame, it is aimed at bringing them and all the peoples of the earth to the City of God, our only lasting home and our eternal rest. God is creator and humanity brick-layers, but to an end that we all rest in a world even now the temple of God, whom we hope one day to see face to face for all eternity.